SYLVAIN ZELLIOT

D1359292

THE GUIDE TO FRIENDSHIP AND SOCIAL COMMUNICATION

Easy Little Routines for Introverted and Atypical People

Translated by
Astra d'Oudney

THE GUIDE TO FRIENDSHIP AND SOCIAL COMMUNICATION

Easy Little Routines for

Introverted and Atypical People

— by —

SYLVAIN ZELLIOT

Translated by
Astra d'Oudney
www.scorpiotraduction.com

Author French Version: Copyright © Sylvain Zelliot, 2020. All rights reserved. English Translation: Copyright © Astra d'Oudney, 2021. All rights reserved.

The cover of this book was designed using Freepik.com resources.

Illustrations (diagrams, characters, icons) by Alexandre Rasamimanana, graphic designer. © 2020.

All rights reserved. This book may not be reproduced, transmitted, distributed or adapted, in whole or part in any form, without prior written permission. Quotations and short excerpts are permitted in reviews for the public press provided that appropriate attribution to this book, its ISBN and author are given.

THE GUIDE TO FRIENDSHIP AND SOCIAL COMMUNICATION - EASY LITTLE ROUTINES FOR INTROVERTED AND ATYPICAL PEOPLE is available from Amazon.com and other Amazon sites.
ISBN : 9798734278857

Website: www.promethee-devperso.com
STANDARD ENGLISH SPELLING

"What matters is not to live like others, but amongst others."
Daniel Tammet

Table of Contents

PRACTICAL INFO SHEETS

AUTHOR'S PREFACE

A Plea for Less Exclusion and More Social Harmony

Communicating, interacting with others and having friends should be the most natural thing in the world, in the same way as eating and sleeping. In ancient times, Aristotle had already observed that man is a social creature, and far more so than the bee or any animal living in a herd, as he is the sole being blessed with speech and culture. By this, he meant that sociability was an integral part of being a human being. There are no random elements in nature. If man is the only species capable of speech, it is with the aim of communicating and living with his fellow human beings. Since the dawn of time, even in the most remote regions of the globe, humans have always gathered together in societies or small tribes.

However, for most of us, communicating or forming relationships is not as easy as it seems! Whether it is living with one's family, working with one's colleagues or going out with one's friends, not a day goes by where we could say, *"I have no need to communicate today."* Indeed no, social communication is a part of daily life and one would even be tempted to say that it is the principal obstacle to achieving happiness.

Five years ago, whilst reflecting on these matters, I met Sebastian and Lucy each separately in a Parisian café for a one-on-one coaching session. They had called on my services to talk to me about their problems in forming relationships. Sebastian and I sat down on the terrace under a beautiful sunny sky. I noticed the tension in his smile as he began to drink his coffee. He spoke in a very low tone of voice as if he did not want the people around to hear us. Yet, our conversation was casual. We talked mostly about his job. As for when I met Lucy, she was chatty and in a positive mood, telling me lots of anecdotes about her childhood, her travels and encounters. However, she did explain to me that she felt a lot less at ease in certain social situations, such as at parties with friends.

Sebastian was a thirty-five-year-old accountant in an IT firm. As a result of loneliness and his shyness issues, he was not happy with his life. He had already read around fifty books on personal development, taken drama and meditation classes, and undergone a slew of therapies as well as interminable sessions with psychoanalysts. It was all to no avail. So, extremely reserved in character, he remained withdrawn at work and had a huge complex when comparing himself with his extrovert colleagues. Sebastian had a pessimistic nature, being convinced that he was incapable of forming any relationship and that nobody was interested in him. Deep down, he would so dearly have loved to find people with whom he could share fun times and form a great friendship, but he did not know how to relate to other people.

Conversely, twenty-seven-year-old Lucy was not shy and led a peaceful life as a student in humanities at the Sorbonne where she had fitted in well. She found it easy to approach others but did not always see the point in doing so, preferring sincere, profound discussion. Lucy considered herself to be an introverted, hypersensitive person. Nevertheless, at parties with friends, she exhausted herself psychologically by trying desperately to keep up conversations and laughing along with others. She felt so terribly frustrated by this predicament that it ended up affecting her morale and discouraging her from repeating this type of experience.

As with many people of their generation, Sebastian and Lucy swore by books on personal development and psychology for learning how to improve their well-being. Both of them had as bedtime reading *How to Win Friends and Influence People* by Dale Carnegie, author of the worldwide bestseller published in 1936. He had written a highly ambitious work, a reference in the field of personal development; one might say a sort of bible of human relations. He had enumerated thirty basic principles pivotal to having success in one's social relationships. Amongst these were secret techniques for becoming a leader, influencing others, gaining sympathy from one's inner circle, and rallying others to one's point of view. Although this book dates from almost a century ago, it still remains a 'must' in our bookshops and contains all the classic tips and tricks repeated in thousands of other self-help books published every year across the world. Be positive, be sociable, have confidence in yourself, and you will make many friends. This is the same old 'stuff' being pumped out today by articles in psychology magazines and lifestyle blogs.

Inspired by Dale Carnegie, Sebastian and Lucy secretly dreamed of becoming sociable people and having lots of friends. They were obsessed with the idea of 'healing' and were convinced their happiness involved eradicating their shyness and introversion. Their eyes gleamed as they asked me whether there were remedies to their mental blocks. I replied that since they had already expended so much effort in well-being therapy and not seen any true progress, it quite simply meant one cannot change everything. To tell the truth, there are things in life on which we can have no effect, such as our personality and innermost nature. It is best to come to terms with them sagaciously. There are others which we can affect, such as one's social communication that can indeed be improved. There is a major difference. I told each of them that the main thing is not to be like others but instead to learn how to live more harmoniously with people whilst still being oneself. The key to this success is social communication. It is the language of nature created to connect human beings with each other. We just need to recapture it so that we can fit in.

Sebastian and Lucy looked interested though sceptical, in response to what I was saying. So, I handed them a manuscript dotted about with notes, personal musings and diagrams of social routines which I had started to draft. It was a kind of mini-guide of social communication taking a new, innovative approach inspired by the science of human ethology and which runs counter to the flood of self-help and psychology books. It was the result of several years' work and research aimed at finding solutions to help people in difficulty fit into society better through learning universal social codes. I wanted Sebastian and Lucy to read it carefully at home so that they could develop a practical understanding of what I was trying to tell them. Above all, I wanted them to follow the advice provided in the manuscript.

As a matter of fact, I had been coaching shy, introverted, hypersensitive and atypical people for around ten years. I had come to the realisation that the advice given by most self-help books is not at all suitable for that segment of the population with an atypical psychological profile, and not even for people in general. First of all, let us be very clear on the following point: most of these types of people do not desperately want to become someone positive, sociable, extroverted and charismatic because, deep down, they feel that this transformation would not be in keeping with their innermost personality. They just want to manage to mix in at work, communicate in a harmonious way with others, and find friends they can count on. These are their simple aspirations for happiness.

On the other hand, we must come to a realistic, honest conclusion: while a condition or feeling of unease can be treated, it can never be completely cured; still less can this be achieved swiftly. A lack of self-confidence, fear of rejection, anxiety and personal traumas are complex and extremely delicate psychological problems. Perhaps the deep sense of being 'different' which a person feels in relation to others is inherent to their personality and inner nature. Under no circumstances can an introverted, anxious or hypersensitive person change their character and resolve their psychological blocks in just a matter of a few months. Not all of us are created equal when it comes to resilience. Anybody who has had the experience of mixing with these sorts of people knows that it takes a tremendous amount of time, possibly years of therapy and self-help, if not a lifetime. In truth, disorders intrinsic to our personality and physiology are often more bearable when we accept them wisely and calmly. We can learn to live with them instead of wearing ourselves out using whatever means to eradicate them.

From this double observation, we come to appreciate more deeply that most of the *leitmotivs* in fashion, "be positive, be sociable, have confidence in yourself," are quite simply inadequate and might even annoy those concerned! What is more, if in addition we have to wait to be healed and overcome all our mental blocks merely to achieve a normal emotional and social life, then we might have a long wait on our hands!

It is at this point Aristotle's observation takes on its full meaning and it is good to remind oneself that man is first and foremost a social creature. Communicating, making friends and forming relationships should be the most natural thing in the world. This assertion might appear a bit obvious but it is just a question of common sense. Each month, every one of us may meet new people through our work, social circle or when we go out. If we take the trouble to abide by the rules of the social game, at any time, we can easily form wonderful human relationships or meet nice people. Often, it only depends on applying a few social routines!

Nature has its own universal social codes. It can be compared with the musical realm in which every human being within their community has their score to play in the orchestra. It is akin to a collection of gestures and notes which harmonise with one another so that the music can be played. Some notes might clash with others or cause unease, such as avoiding eye contact, prolonged silences, stammering, and so on. However, human beings will always be receptive to a lovely chord or to appealing social communication – this is in humans' nature as social creatures. To those who know how to show signs of sociability, this might take the form of a smile, a kind word, empathy, or a friendly gesture… Often, this is what can connect with people and allows one to be in harmony with the group despite a disability or being 'different'! Knowing these rules means a person can grasp the game of social interactions more easily and find the means to create a bridge to reach out to others.

A few weeks later, I met up with Sebastian and Lucy again on the same café terrace, but this time they had smiles on their faces and a bright, jolly look. "*I had a real Eureka moment!*" said Sebastian to me. Furthermore, Lucy sounded so relieved as she told me, "*Ah! I can now talk to people in a straightforward, relaxed way, thanks to those little routines.*"

Of course, they did not become sociable people in everyday life all of a sudden. Sebastian and Lucy had now got the picture that they always would have a certain amount of leeway in the way they interacted with others, depending on how they used social communication. Sebastian had been suffering from loneliness and was convinced that nobody was interested in him. However, he now realised that he often did receive friendly openings from those in his social circle. It was just that he had not recognised them as such up to that point, and had regularly been missing out on opportunities to make friends. Similarly, Lucy had found out that she too could escape her fate, rather than automatically blaming her social difficulties on psychological blocks. She now knew that at any time she could use a few little routines to help herself handle particular anxiety-provoking social situations, such as conversations at parties, or more private moments when it comes to forming true relationships. The main thing was not being sociable or talkative, but rather to use suitable social communication. Sebastian and Lucy had become aware of all this thanks to my manuscript.

From that came my idea of making the manuscript into an extremely ambitious book to share the content with as many people as possible. It would be a handbook of social communication based on knowledge and application of the universal rules governing social interactions; a sort of "*handbook for people who are 'different'*," to handle every social situation which might be problematic on a one-to-one or group basis.

I firmly believe in the betterment of our world through social routines and that if everyone applied the book's basic principles, there would definitely be less exclusion and more social harmony between human beings.

This book is a guide which will make it possible for you to take a few more steps towards your own personal self-fulfilment. The first theoretical part is essential for you to acquire basic knowledge, and understand what is going on in your social interactions. The second section is practical and given over to info sheets and real-life examples. The book cannot make the journey for you, but it will provide you with the keys to making your social communication a success whilst staying true to who you are.

Sylvain Zelliot

INTRODUCTION

BASIC CONCEPTS TO HELP YOU GET STARTED AND GAIN A GOOD UNDERSTANDING

1) WHAT IS SOCIAL COMMUNICATION?

Social communication refers to a person's set of social skills for connecting with others.

In plain language, it is the type of communication you use every day to interact with other people or for forming a friendly relationship!

Social communication can be verbal (your words) or non-verbal (your gestures and facial expressions).

Whether you are at work or going out at the weekend, the success or otherwise of these following aspects depends on your social communication:

Achieving integration into a group, social relations, friendship, etc.

Therefore, paying attention to one's social communication is essential in order to live in harmony with others.

What one has to remember is that social communication is universal. It is a prerequisite for all forms of interaction between species.

Without social communication, human beings could not make contact with each other!

Social communication also exists amongst animals. Each creature has its own social codes to make contact with its fellow animals.

For example, the dolphin whistles to alert other dolphins when it is in distress. A dog sends signals by yapping, wagging its tail and moving its paws forward as an invitation to other dogs to play.

Amongst humans, social communication appears at birth. It is a common misconception that it develops with language.

However, right from the outset, prelinguistic social communication already emerges between the baby and its parents: smiling, vocal exchanges, facial expressions, egocentric speech,[1] and so forth. Smiling even appears in children who are born deaf and blind.

Acquiring social skills is part of the individual's overall development from childhood to adulthood. It gives structure to all his or her social communication.

2) SOCIAL COMMUNICATION: HALFWAY BETWEEN INSTINCT AND LEARNING…

Our social communication is a construct deriving from a perfect blend of instinct and learning.

Approaching another person with whom we wish to interact, making eye contact during a conversation, and respecting a certain physical distance are instinctive social skills.

This is part of the biological and social nature of human beings.

Then, throughout the ages and in various cultures, social and cultural codes have developed to accompany these instinctive social skills.

For example, looking someone in the eye and smiling during a conversation are signs of sociability in Western countries. However, this is regarded very differently in some Arab countries or Russian republics, where looking someone in the eye and smiling can be taken as a lack of respect, especially at important meetings!

Depending on the culture, these instinctive social skills have shifted to mean something either positive or negative.

In other particular cases, with the evolution of species by natural selection, instinctive social skills may have been distorted or disorientated by genetic mutations which are the source of certain developmental or behavioural disorders, as are found in autism, Asperger's Syndrome, phobia or social anxiety.

Undoubtedly, the laws of nature have favoured and amplified some adaptive behaviour[2] to ensure the success and survival of the human species and maintain order within society. Examples include the fear of how others perceive you to induce a normalisation of behaviour within a group; anxiety to anticipate danger; obsessional and compulsive behaviour to help hone construction of dwellings in the natural environment, etc.

In any event, whatever the exact reasons, human beings are biologically equipped with a range of human signals (eye contact, smiling, gestures) with which they can interact coherently and harmoniously with others.

Hold on tight!
A little bit of theory is required to understand what's coming next...

Warning: The idea here is not to hold forth about the social origin of man and elaborate on evolutionist theories because this would require a separate book. The intention herein is to provide the reader with a primer in the form of an understandable interpretative framework. Let us simply remember the notion that basically there are universal social skills whose sole aim is to enable any human to interact with his or her fellow humans. We shall come back to this later on when we deal with the concept of signs of sociability.

In this book, we do not aim to tackle the subject of cultural codes or other sociological criteria when meeting people. We do not deny that they exist but the topic is not expanded upon for the reason that cultural codes are specific to each country and, generally speaking, are not an obstacle to our readers connecting positively with others! Social norms, mores and customs are amongst subjects which will not be addressed. Actually, most introverted or shy people have mastered these basics in their interactions with others, but as we shall see in due course, it is their social communication which creates problems! For the purposes of clarity and coherence, we shall focus mainly on this and related topics.

3) CONCISE GLOSSARY OF SOCIAL COMMUNICATION

Throughout the book, we will use vocabulary dedicated to social communication, and diagrams to illustrate ideas presented.

Let us imagine that the two men below, Kevin and Peter, are young arrivals at a new company:

Kevin, 27,   Peter, 36,
graphic designer   accountant

Kevin and Peter are not necessarily aware of it but they bring together a whole set of 'ingredients' which make meeting each other and fitting in at work go smoothly. They have applied their social skills and complied with social and cultural codes... But what is the difference between all these concepts?

To start with, we suggest a simple and general definition built on a new discipline specific to social communication and social interaction:

Social interactionology is the discipline focusing on the study of social communication and implicit codes which govern interactions between individuals.

We provide you with the following glossary of keywords which will be used throughout the book. It is essential for readers to know them if they wish to have a proper understanding and not get lost along the way.

 # GLOSSARY

♦ **Social skills** are a set of instinctive, acquired social abilities which help us communicate with others.

E.g., making eye contact; smiling; listening; greeting people; introducing oneself; thanking, approaching and inviting people are all social skills.

♦ **Human signals** (eye contact, smiling and gestures) are a set of instinctive signs, particular to individuals, which are used to communicate amongst themselves to show interest in a conversation or connect with people.

The act of smiling is a social skill, but to have a smile is a human signal which is used, for example, to show that you are available for a friendly chat!

♦ **Social codes** are a set of implicit rules which one person has to abide by in order to have a coherent, appropriate social interaction with another person.

Cultural codes are a set of officially codified rules with which a person must comply in order to live properly amongst others, depending on which defined group or society they belong to.

E.g., shaking hands or leaning forward are body language gestures which correspond to social greeting codes but relate to two different cultural codes depending on whether you are in Europe or China.

♦ **Self-improvement and social routines** are a set of personal development techniques, tips and tricks intended to develop one's prospects of success in interacting with others.

E.g., saying someone's first name and reiterating their words during a conversation are techniques to show that you take a genuine interest in them.

CHAPTER I

THE BASICS OF SOCIAL COMMUNICATION

HUMAN INTERACTION
AND SIGNS OF AVAILABILITY

1) WHAT IS SUCCESSFUL SOCIAL COMMUNICATION?

Now that all the definitions have been given, let us get to the heart of the matter. Our aim now is to grasp what "successful social communication" actually *is* when you meet people!

We frequently meet new people at work or when we go out at the weekend. Whether it is a new colleague at work, a customer, neighbour or a friend, we must interact with that person properly in order to build a relationship with them.

However, this interaction should not take place in 'any old fashion'! When two people meet each other, to begin with there is a whole set of signals and implicit rules which each person has to heed, in order for everything to go smoothly throughout their conversation.

Social communication is the decisive parameter which will steer you to success or failure in your meetings.

The following diagram shows us the importance of social communication. Many people believe that their personality or physical appearance is the reason why they have limited success in social relationships or get rejected. However, in the majority of cases, it is primarily caused by social communication problems!

It turns out that the other person may feel uncomfortable or distance themselves during a conversation if they see **that you do not interact with them enough or do so in an incorrect manner.**

Remember that this can be seen in the aspects which comprise your social communication: your eye contact, smile, body posture, conversation, and so on.

REASONS FOR SUCCESS AND CAUSES OF FAILURE IN YOUR SOCIAL ENCOUNTERS

Example of **"Successful" Social Communication**	Example of **"Awkward" Social Communication**
- Synchronised eye contact - Communicative smile - Flowing conversation - Open posture; expressive gestures - Taking an interest in the other person, etc.	- Avoids eye contact - Tense smile - Gaps in conversation - Closed posture; crossed arms - No interest in the other person, etc.

↓

Flowing, coherent conversation	**Bewilderment; unease felt by the other person**

↓

Potential outcome depending on affinity: - Formal/informal relationship - Friendly ties	**Potential outcome:** - They continue but are uncomfortable - They cut the conversation short and move away

"Failure is not due to your personality but to flaws in your social communication."

You will see from the diagram above that this is a typical situation which everyone has been through at some time in their life.

When someone looks you in the eye, smiles at you and talks to you, it simply means that they are trying to interact with you.

If the person you are talking to avoids eye contact and does not keep the conversation going, then there is a good chance you will interpret this to mean they are unavailable and it would be preferable for you to interact with someone else in the group who is more likely to communicate with you.

This is a natural, instinctive reaction – people prefer to try to converse with those who interact with them the most.

Those people who are regarded as sociable and who make friends easily achieve such attributes as a result of their active social communication. They have a communicative smile; a candid expression; they can make conversation; and they are proactive, etc.

To gain new awareness, let us look at the next diagram! See next page.

CASE STUDY: TO GAIN AWARENESS, LET'S TAKE A FEW EXTREMES

  COMPARISON

A "HIGHLY SOCIABLE" person	An "ANTISOCIAL" person
↓	↓
Example of **"Appealing" Social Communication**	Example of **"Closed" Social Communication**
- A warm smile - A sincere look - Lively conversation - Friendly gestures, a tap on the shoulder - Interacts with others a great deal: listens, compliments, suggests, etc.	- Does not smile - Does not look at people - No conversation - Hands in pockets - Does not interact with others: ignores them; turns his/her back, etc.

 IMPACT ON ONE'S FRIENDS AND FAMILY

THE "SOCIAL MAGNET" EFFECT	THE "SOCIAL REPULSION" EFFECT
- Draws people to him/her - Is highly attractive at a personal level - Gets asked out - Has a lot of friends	- Repels people - Is unattractive at a personal level - Never gets asked out - Has few, or no friends

From this diagram, we can have a better understanding of the impact that successful or poor social communication has and its indirect consequences on one's friends and family. This is because, quite apart from physical appearance or personality criteria, primarily, what makes people most uncomfortable when they go out with someone is if we do not interact with them sufficiently. This is the particular error to avoid and we cannot blame people for ignoring us if they see we are giving them a frosty look, or we do not speak to them.

There is a compelling logic to social interactions and we cannot deny the following:

> ► **Successful social communication** will always tend to make the speaker likeable, and the other person more willing to communicate with them.
>
> ► **Awkward or inadequate social communication** will tend to undermine the speaker, and make the other person less likely to communicate with them.

Obviously, this is a general pattern but having said that, things do not need to be this way. Making blunders, having mental blocks or being unaware of our deficiencies in communication comprise the common fate of all human beings, whether or not they happen to be particularly shy or introverted. The very purpose of this book is to demonstrate that, in spite of all that, there are indeed solutions to remedy the situation, as we shall see in all subsequent chapters.

2) SIGNS OF AVAILABILITY; SIGNS OF UNAVAILABILITY

As one sees from the previous diagrams, looking a person in the eye or smiling during a conversation are key elements in successful social communication. These are actually human signals. They show a person that you are available to interact with them.

Imagine the following scene: you are invited to a social or other type of function (a party, a conference, a training course). You arrive in a room filled with people and you do not know anyone. What happens logically in this type of situation?

The first people you notice are those who smile at you and speak to you. Instinctively, you head towards the people who appear available to interact with you. You notice all these signs, thanks to their behaviour.

Conversely, you pay less attention to people in the room who stay in their corner and do not look towards you, including those only a few inches away from you but who have their arms crossed or look occupied.

That is exactly what is going on in the mind of a person who is deciding whether to interact with you or not. **They look for your signs of availability before anything else.**

To grasp these fundamental concepts, we suggest you have a look at the following chart and compare each type of behaviour.

Examples of Signs of Availability:	Examples of Signs of Unavailability:
Candid expression; looking interested	Avoiding eye contact; head down
Clear voice; making conversation	Low or inaudible voice; remains wordless
Communicative, friendly smile	No smile or a tense smile
Open body posture; expressive gestures	Crossed arms; hands in pockets; seems busy or preoccupied
Communicative state of mind	Timid, aloof or stern demeanour
Approaches the person on their territory; makes the first move	Takes no initiatives: passive demeanour; stays in their corner
Responsiveness to friendly propositions	Answers "no" or "some other time" to friendly propositions

In fact, at evenings out, it can happen that some people are never approached, or they can even be completely abandoned by the other guests in attendance. How can we explain this?

There is a simple reason – **these people express signs of unavailability through their behaviour.**

With their 'closed-off' demeanour, unbeknownst to them, they either appear unapproachable or not very approachable. They give others the impression that they are unavailable. As a result, people do not think to interact with them. Personality, physical appearance and age are not the primary causes of exclusion at social events, contrary to what some people might believe!

It is a matter of social ethology and biological behaviour. Humans instinctively sense availability or unavailability signals in the behaviour of their fellow human beings. They are more inclined to interact with individuals who appear available. Such are the laws of nature.

Moreover, even at a social outing with shy or introverted people, just because the people are of a similar disposition does not necessarily mean they are more sympathetic and will help each other fit in. The same laws apply here too. Those who display the fewest signs of availability will have the greatest likelihood of being excluded from the group. Quite simply, a person who does not speak or interact does not give others the opportunity to connect with them.

Therefore, we shall take on board the following two definitions:

Signs of Availability: These indicate a person's friendly demeanour in appearing available and approachable for others to talk to. Examples: a smile; looking interested; listening. We refer to this type of social communication as being "open."

Signs of Unavailability: These indicate a person's wilful or involuntary demeanour in appearing unavailable for others to speak to. Examples: avoiding eye contact; no smile; occupied-looking posture. We refer to this type of social communication as being "closed."

Here are several examples of everyday situations to get a proper insight and serve as your 'wake-up call':

Situation 1: *Your preoccupied appearance is a sign of unavailability*

No doubt, you will have already experienced problems fitting in with fellow students or co-workers when you took tea breaks at university or work. At some time or other, precisely because you did not want to seem uncomfortable in public or give the impression of being alone, you subconsciously took up a lot of little habits which ran contrary to your initial desire to fit in. During these tea breaks, you now pretend to be busy all the time, to be deep in thought, to tap away at your smartphone, to keep going back and forth down corridors with your files... when deep down, actually, you are feeling disconcerted.

This is a mistake, for, in so doing, you display signs of unavailability to others and reduce your chances of fitting in!

Situation 2: *Your extremely reserved character is the underlying cause of your signs of unavailability*

At work, your colleagues praise your skills and professionalism. In short, you do a very good job but you have the misfortune of realising that you are always the last person to be told about what is going on in the life of the company – a change of schedule; a cancelled meeting; an important forthcoming event, and so on. As usual, all your colleagues already know all about it, but not you. They are invited to noontime drinks at lunch, but not you; they receive nice thoughtful little gifts, but not you... Yet, you are good-looking; always punctual and you do outstanding work. So, why are you excluded? Undoubtedly, it is because you do not interact or communicate socially with others enough. Nor do you accept their invitations. Your highly reserved, serious disposition can be interpreted as a sign of unavailability.

Situation 3: *Your psychological hang-ups are the underlying cause of your signs of unavailability*

A business of around fifty employees throws a party for the staff with cocktails and a buffet on the terrace. Patrick, a forty-something cleaner, feels a bit out of place amongst all these young executives in suits and ties. As he starts to get psychologically hung-up comparing himself with the others, he lowers his head and retreats into himself, unwittingly activating signs of unavailability. That is the big mistake – he will make himself invisible to everyone else. Yes, his particular status already does not help him stand out. Yet, this is not an AGM but a time for partying and sharing! By first showing signs of availability (smiling, forcing oneself to approach others), and then going and talking with people and taking a genuine interest in them, Patrick would then hold all the cards allowing him to fit in successfully. This is because human beings, whatever their status or background, will always be receptive to another person's kindness, to a sincere smile, and to "appealing social communication."

Let us have a look at the next diagram which helps you memorise the fundamentals!

SIGNS OF AVAILABILITY
IN SOCIAL SITUATIONS

REMEMBER!
When you're with others, your first
question should be:

DO I DISPLAY THESE
SIGNS OF
AVAILABILITY?
> A candid look
> A smile
> A clear voice
> Open body posture
> An approachable demeanour
> I approach the other person

The General Rule: People are attracted first by those whose behaviour displays signs of availability.
Conversely, they will be more aloof with those whose behaviour displays signs of unavailability.

CHAPTER II

"IDEAL" SOCIAL COMMUNICATION AS ADVOCATED BY DALE CARNEGIE

1) DALE CARNEGIE'S THIRTY PRINCIPLES OF SOCIABILITY

When it comes to discussion of human relationships, there is a certain book one cannot avoid talking about. You are sure to have heard of the famous bestseller, *How to Win Friends and Influence People*[3] by American writer Dale Carnegie, published in 1936. Almost a century later, millions of copies continue to be sold across the world. It is a cult classic often found in the Personal Development and Human Relationships sections of bookshops. Whether you realise it or not, you will have definitely come across it already, be it at a shopping centre or in a friend's bookcase!

In the book, Dale Carnegie set himself the huge challenge of studying and revealing all the universal ingredients required to enjoy success in social relationships. It is a sort of manual proffering a list of Thirty Principles which hinge on the following pivotal ideas, namely, becoming sociable; influencing others; gaining people's sympathy; rallying others to your point of view; becoming a leader, and so forth. So, it is no wonder that this book has become a reference for millions of people fascinated by communication and personal development.

To get an idea, let us summarise Dale Carnegie's Thirty Principles:

1. Don't criticise, condemn or complain.
2. Give honest and sincere appreciation.
3. Arouse in the other person an eager want.
4. Become genuinely interested in other people.
5. Smile.
6. Remember that a person's name is to that person the sweetest and most important sound in any language.
7. Be a good listener. Encourage others to talk about themselves.
8. Talk in terms of the other person's interests.
9. Make the other person feel important – and do it sincerely.
10. The only way to get the best of an argument is to avoid it.
11. Show respect for the other person's opinions. Never say, "You're wrong."

12. If you are wrong, admit it quickly and emphatically.
13. Begin in a friendly way.
14. Get the other person saying "yes, yes" immediately.
15. Let the other person do a great deal of the talking.
16. Let the other person feel that the idea is his or hers.
17. Try honestly to see things from the other person's point of view.
18. Be sympathetic with the other person's ideas and desires.
19. Appeal to the nobler motives.
20. Dramatise your ideas.
21. Throw down a challenge.
22. Begin with praise and honest appreciation.
23. Call attention to people's mistakes indirectly.
24. Talk about your own mistakes before criticising the other person.
25. Ask questions instead of giving direct orders.
26. Let the other person save face.
27. Praise the slightest improvement and praise every improvement. Be "hearty in your approbation and lavish in your praise."
28. Give the other person a fine reputation to live up to.
29. Use encouragement. Make the fault seem easy to correct.
30. Make the other person happy about doing the thing you suggest.

Source: Principles taken from How to Win Friends and Influence People by Dale Carnegie.

2) IS THE DALE CARNEGIE METHOD SUITABLE FOR EVERYONE?

The type of social communication proposed by Dale Carnegie is what one could call a form of "ideal" or "optimal social communication" relevant to any person wishing to enjoy success in their human relationships.

Everything you have to do to please others in order to build a relationship swiftly – in an *ideal* situation – has been brought together in this list.

In the list, you will recognise a whole set of sociability signals we shall refer to in the following chapters, which are natural components of social attraction between two people. These include: *smiling; taking a sincere interest in others; knowing how to be conciliatory; expressing one's gratitude, etc.*

To this may be added masses of other little routines which are human or friendly techniques to maximise the likelihood of social attraction. These include: *being positive; never saying someone is wrong; praising the slightest improvement and praising every improvement; avoiding controversy, and so on.*

Actually, this form of social communication does make use of all the modern mainstays of personal development. These are stereotypical recommendations which today we find in books on personal development and seduction!

So, it is for good reason that Dale Carnegie is considered as a pioneer of the entire realm of personal development literature.

Do these techniques work? Of course they do, because anyone who puts these thirty principles into practice will definitely enjoy greater success and win friends in return. People are always more receptive and sympathetic towards a person who is positive and gives them praise. However, that is not the issue. The real question is the following:

Is it healthy to adopt this type of social communication with people on a daily basis?

Unfortunately, some of the advice Dale Carnegie recommends leads one to believe that, in order to build a harmonious relationship, it is always best to remain positive, conciliatory, and to exploit influencing techniques to achieve one's ends. The game of social appearances seems to take precedence over everything. The advice should be followed with moderation as otherwise it might lead to hypocritical behaviour or encourage role-playing.

This form of social communication is generally used by politicians, entrepreneurs and salespeople. That is normal. Most of the time, such individuals move in a professional context wherein the goal is to please and influence people, behave in a diplomatic fashion with customers, and negotiate contracts.

Still, the Dale Carnegie method, however effective it might be, is arguably not appropriate for all audiences and individuals, including introverted, reserved and hypersensitive people; or more broadly, all those who value sincerity in human relationships.

It is crucial to stress how important it is *not* to follow all of Carnegie's advice to the letter, and to call upon one's common sense too!

Throughout this book, we shall examine a new form of social communication which is more suitable for introverted personalities.

CHAPTER III

FITTING IN WITH OTHERS

1) THE NEED FOR SOCIAL BELONGING

The need for social belonging is natural to human beings.[4] It reflects an individual's need to make friends and feel integrated within a community. Anyone who lives in society harbours deep within themselves the dread of not being accepted by others.

We cannot deny it – the feeling of being integrated within a group generates positive emotions, such as happiness and tranquillity; whereas, the feeling of exclusion engenders negative emotions, such as solitude, angst and depression.

Every renowned scientific study[5] on the subject establishes a connection between isolation and mental health. These range from the famous book and study, *Suicide*, by Durkheim in 1897 (which highlights the strong statistical connection between isolation and the risk of suicide), up to more recent research by Bowlby in 1970 into attachment and newborns' anxiety when separated from their family.

At the very least, all human beings want to surround themselves with friends with whom they can share leisure pursuits and on whom they can rely in life. Whether it is at work, school or at a party, our primary and ultimate goal is to satisfy that biological need for social belonging.

In spite of that, building relationships is a tricky task when we do not possess the necessary social codes due to self-confidence issues or an unawareness of our shortcomings in communication. When you start to meet people on a regular basis, you create a lot of opportunities to forge new relationships. There is something you might not have noticed at work, your sports' club, or in your inbox – yet this is the first important item to point out, so that 'the penny drops': people do make friendly advances to connect with you and get to know you better from an amicable perspective.

In fact, it is practically impossible for you not to have had some sort of an invitation or suggestion of a friendly outing, because every human being, whatever their background, instinctively seeks to connect with others. In order to make friends, the first reaction we must have is to start 'seeing' the friendly advances which people make towards us on a daily basis!

THINGS TO CONTEMPLATE

What does the biggest study ever into happiness conducted by Harvard reveal?

Having a nice job, becoming rich or famous... what can make a person truly happy?

Scientists from Harvard University[6] wondered about the secrets of happiness and embarked on an incredible study in 1938. To this end, they observed the daily lives of 724 men for... 75 years! One half of the panel was chosen from the élite of students at Harvard and the other half from the poor quarters of Boston. Over the years, successive researchers have meticulously questioned the human subjects about their work, family and state of health. Every detail, however small, has been gone over with a 'fine-tooth comb', using such tools as satisfaction surveys; testimony from relatives; blood analyses; brain scanners, and so on.

In 2015, psychiatrist Robert Waldinger published the findings of this monumental study, initiated three quarters of a century ago and of which he is the fourth Director. Some of the men studied went on to become lawyers, doctors and labourers, whilst others became alcoholics and schizophrenics.

He has observed that those individuals most connected socially with their friends, family and community are happier, enjoy better health and live longer than those who are less connected.

Loneliness accelerates ageing of the brain and memory decline. Isolated people are less happy; their state of health declines in middle age and they die at a younger age. Furthermore, the quality of close relationships seems to take precedence over the quantity of friends or whether or not there is a marital relationship. Conflict is bad for health. It is better to be alone than in a poor relationship. Those people who were most satisfied in their relationships at the age of 50 were the healthiest at 80.

The findings of this study are crystal clear: good social relationships guarantee happiness, health and memory.

Social ties are also a condition for happiness. When a person achieves social harmony, not only do they live a more fulfilled life but a longer one too. The message is also reassuring for introverted people. It is not the number of friends which matters but the quality of relationships. To be happy in life, all one needs in the end are a few close relationships and some people you can count on.

2) WHAT IS A FRIENDLY ADVANCE?

In social communication, making a friendly advance to somebody is, by definition, an action with an implicit intention to connect with another person.

For example, you go out and meet someone. You have an enjoyable conversation together and have a very good feeling about them, but there is a strong likelihood that you will never meet this person again in the future. Making a friendly advance is simply an externalisation of one's amicable interest, with the aim of getting to know that person better and connecting with them.

Even at work, school or in the canteen, people make friendly advances to you and give you the opportunity to build or strengthen a relationship. However, perhaps you are not aware of it. 'Seeing' these friendly advances could change your life and allow you to develop more satisfactory, harmonious social relationships!

Most of the time, friendly advances are to be found in your conversations with people. Here is a practical chart with examples of everyday conversations. Amongst other things, it will help you do the following:

➢ Be aware of the friendly advances people might make towards you.

➢ Get some ideas yourself for friendly advances you might make to others.

Examples of Friendly Advances:	What this might indicate:
What are your hobbies?	The person would like to know you better and discover whether you share the same interests...
What are you doing this weekend?	The person wants to know your hobbies or find out whether you're available to go out together...
Would you like a cup of tea?	Your work colleague is making a friendly

How about a croissant?	advance in order to strike up a conversation with you…
How would you like to come to the drinks party on Friday?	Your work colleague is suggesting you meet in a more light-hearted, convivial setting to talk about things other than work...
Got any ideas where we could go out next time?	The person is proffering you an opening so that you can meet up again…
I'm throwing a games party at my place tomorrow. So, if you'd like to come along...	This is obviously a friendly invitation!
What's your number?	The person liked you and would like to have your number to stay in touch…
What's your Facebook page?	The person wants to add you to their list of friends…

Obviously, these examples and their interpretations are not to be taken literally. It is up to you to be perceptive and notice the nuances; for instance, by differentiating between advances which are of the friendly or the romantic type; and utterances that have no specific purpose other than to keep the conversation going and avoid gaps. Friendly advances are generally more neutral and less insistent than romantic advances!

Three important questions to ask yourself in the event of social failure

As by now you will have realised, friendly advances made by people are an invitation to get to know you better and to build a relationship with you. They are an excuse to see you again by suggesting you go out together.

Nevertheless, if you are still finding it hard to make friends or are still alone despite meeting many people, you should ask yourself the following questions:

THE THREE QUESTIONS "FRIENDSHIP TEST"

✓ *Do I see or am I aware of any friendly advances people make to me?*

✓ *Do I respond positively or do I tend to ignore or respond negatively to every invitation?*

✓ *Have I myself made friendly advances to people I've met? And, if so, how many specifically?*

If the reply is "no" to each question, it is logical for you to feel that nobody is making you friendly advances to go out at the weekend. The truth is that perhaps you did not pay enough attention to them and it is not because nobody is thinking of you!

You are bound to have received friendly advances if you go out from time to time and meet people.

Why? Because it is in human nature to show oneself to be at least a little bit sociable and build social ties. Even at a special outing between shy people, they will create openings to get to know each other better, extend a conversation, and see each other again. Also, at the end of an outing or event, before people take their leave of each other, it is usual for them to make approaches so that they can meet up again at another time.

As for romantic advances, evidently we agree that it is pretty rare to get those every week from people of the opposite sex, unless, of course we are blessed with extremely good looks!

However, when it comes to friendly advances... as soon as you start meeting people regularly, it is quite simply unlikely, if not impossible, for you not to receive any approaches.

3) FRIENDLY ADVANCES AND SIGNS OF AVAILABILITY

It is quite true that some people receive more friendly advances than others, and that some receive hardly any at all even though they put a lot of effort into meeting people and going out. This might seem unfair to the latter group, but they need to understand deeper reasons in order for them to have the opportunity to reverse the trend! In the following chapters, we shall attempt to figure out why some people receive more friendly advances and invitations than others at the same social event.

You already know the principal reason why some people instinctively do not come over to you at an event or party. Remind yourself of Chapter I – it is primarily due to your signs of unavailability. The same goes for friendly advances. If you do not show yourself to be sufficiently available to people, then there is no likelihood of their wanting to interact with you.

Imagine that you go to a special event, party or an after-work do and arrive in a room full of people. Always remember to display your signs of availability to people, as shown in the following diagram.

SIGNS OF AVAILABILITY AT DATES, EVENTS AND PARTIES

Paul finds himself amongst other people...

Signs of Availability	**Signs of Unavailability**
1) He approaches the other person	1) He doesn't take the initiative
2) Open expression	2) Avoids eye contact
3) Communicative smile	3) No smile or tense smile
4) Clear voice	4) Low voice
5) Open body posture	5) Head down; arms crossed
6) Positive, welcoming demeanour	6) Aloof, preoccupied demeanour
Paul shows himself to be available 'on the scene'	Paul tries to make himself invisible
He gives people the opportunity of chatting and making friendly advances to him!	**He doesn't give people the opportunity of chatting or making friendly advances to him!**

In the previous diagram, we have set out a list of signs of availability in order of importance. Obviously, the idea is not to abide by all of them at once when you are in company but at least to follow the essential ones.

For example, if you are not a bubbly sort of person and afraid of seeming 'invisible' to others because of your naturally reticent character, remember that when you approach other people first, you immediately show yourself to be available to them whatever happens.

You always have a certain amount of leeway and if people do not make friendly advances to you, bear in mind that you still have the option of doing it yourself by making sociable advances to others!

Remember! Generally speaking, the same is true in life. Be it at work or with your friends and family, if you always appear to be occupied or withdrawn, people will automatically interpret that you are not available and soon grow weary of extending invitations to you.

4) OVERCOMING EXCLUSION WITH APPEARANCE AND PERSONALITY

There is another significant reason explaining why some people have less social success than others when they go out, and they tend to be held in lower regard. This is due to the phenomenon of **negative social labelling**.

Yes, sometimes, before even triggering our signs of availability, people may have already made up their minds as to whether they are going to interact with us or move away; that is to say, whether they want to connect with us or keep their distance!

That is what happens every time people meet each other. We make the acquaintance of someone new and we tend to label them all too peremptorily by putting them in 'pigeonholes':

"Too young or too old; effeminate or gay; pleasant or awkward; serious or highbrow; introverted or withdrawn; disabled or fragile; poverty-stricken or 'loaded'; weird or crazy, and so on."

If we find the person to be too much inclined this or that way, we keep our distance, hold our tongue, and choose to interact with another person who finds favour with us. All of this is regrettable, of course, but it is human nature and everyone does it without thinking twice.

We must not deny this reality: there are qualities and personality traits which are more attractive than others and more highly valued depending on culture and the influence of stereotypes in society.

When people are good-looking, rich, exude charisma and have an engaging personality, they have a substantially higher chance of receiving friendly advances than if they have a physically unprepossessing appearance, are introverted or live with a disability.

This is certainly the case, but nothing is written in stone in the social world.

All these various obstacles are not as insurmountable as in the romantic realm where it is often a matter of serious commitment between two people; a decision to live as a couple. Mostly, we choose our friends based on the affinity we have for them and the enjoyment we get from being in their company!

Example of a RESOLVED negative social labelling situation!

24-year-old Anthony goes to a student party at his university for the first time. He has brown hair, round glasses and a face slightly disfigured from a bicycle accident. He senses that his appearance might make people feel uncomfortable. Most do avoid him or pretend not to notice him, for that matter. In this instance, Anthony is the victim of negative social labelling due to his physical appearance (his face) and his personality (he is rather highbrow).

Problem: If Anthony remains passive and stays in his corner, the negative social labelling phenomenon will be exacerbated in people's minds. Consequently, he will make himself hard to approach.

A recommended solution: Anthony will give himself a tremendous opportunity if he activates his signs of availability first (i.e., he approaches others), and then socialises with people. For example, Anthony introduces himself to others and talks a bit about himself, sharing some nice, amusing anecdotes. He then discovers that he has things in common with some of the guests who, pleasantly surprised, try to find out more about his hobbies...

In this case, Anthony's successful social communication has made it possible to switch negative social labelling to positive social labelling. People have opened up to him, leaving their prejudices aside, and learning to discover his personality. This is what happens in everyday life. Most people who have off-putting, little shortcomings or a disability manage to build relationships because they are the ones to make the first move towards others and strike up conversation. This forces the others gradually to get rid of their bias.

That is why social communication is so important in meetings, as shown by the following diagram! See next page.

KEY FACTORS IN YOUR SOCIAL ENCOUNTERS

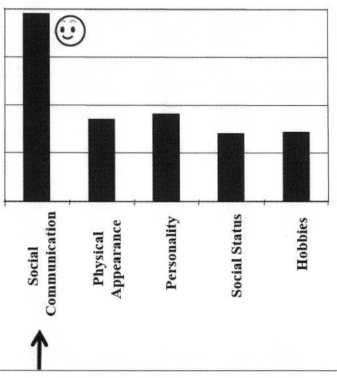

Proficient social communication compensates for inadequacies in other areas.

A plain-looking, unemployed yet highly sociable man will always be more "attractive" than a handsome, brilliant but antisocial fellow!

The key point for you to remember is that successful social communication allows you to bypass certain preconceptions and gives you leeway with people, as summarised by the table below:

Negative social labelling can relate to:	Potential discriminatory situations:	REMEMBER!
Appearance (age, ethnic origin, physical appearance, disability, etc.)	- Public places - Meetings, outings - Celebrations, parties - At work - Job interviews - At school or university	"Successful social communication" can also: ➔ **replace** a person's appearance or demeanour; ➔ create **positive labelling** instead.
Demeanour (your personality, shyness, highbrow, effeminate, mannerisms, etc.)		

5) THE BEST WAY TO APPEAR AVAILABLE: APPROACH PEOPLE

A friend of yours is organising a barbecue party on the terrace of his house and is happy to invite you along. When you get there, you see around twenty guests and do not know a single one with the exception of your host. You want to fit in amongst the guests as swiftly as possible. Let us recap one last time on the basic reactions you should have and which will make you appear available to other people at the party:

The 6 signals which inform people as to your availability or otherwise: ⚠		Signs of Availability: *Everything is very active: People see you!*
1) Venturing into other people's territory	=>	**I approach the other person**
2) Eye contact	=>	I have a candid expression
3) Smile	=>	I smile
4) Voice	=>	I have a clear voice; I speak
5) Body posture	=>	I make expressive gestures
6) State of mind	=>	I have a communicative demeanour

In a room full of people, those who smile most are the first to be approached because smiling is a strong sign of availability and non-hostility. In fact, when you see someone smile, you are reassured and think to yourself that they are available to interact with you. That is why a communicative smile is effective.

Nevertheless – and it is vital to point this out – if you are not the smiling type or are rather tense and extremely awkward in spite of your efforts, it is not the end of the world! In order for you not to come up empty-handed at the party, the main thing to remember is this:

The most decisive action will always be to approach the other person first

The best way to induce social interactions is to approach other people yourself. You oblige them to interact with you and under no circumstances will they reject you, either out of social instinct or the obligations of courtesy.

Whether it is a cocktail party at a professional event or a student party, the more you approach people, the more you increase your chances of collecting business cards from future collaborators or phone numbers of potential friends. Quite simply, nothing will happen if you do not approach anyone.

Approaching people is the most important thing because, if no one comes up to you, it is you who must create the meeting situation by making the first move towards the other person.

If you go out on a social jaunt to the banks of the Thames and you only chat to one person out of the six people present, you might make a nice acquaintance or even perhaps a friend if you are lucky.

However, if you take a few minutes to approach every one of the six people and try to get to know them, then you will truly have interacted with the group and brought about a number of opportunities to build relationships.

This is logical – you have to grasp all this from the social ethology angle. When you venture into another person's territory, you make yourself available and the individual you are talking to is obliged out of social instinct to make him or herself available to you in turn and interact with you.

Taking the initiative is also a solution to lift yourself out of negative social labelling. We saw this with Anthony in the previous example where, at a party, people who have not even met you have already negatively labelled you and dare not come over to chat.

Approaching people first means that they can get to know you, which helps them leave their prejudices behind.

> **Remember!** Ultimately, whether or not you appear anxious or awkward when you approach someone is not really of great importance, as long as you have made that first move towards someone else. How the interaction with them progresses and natural affinity will decide where the relationship goes from there.

Approaching others provides you with a lot of room for manoeuvre:

On one hand, whether a social interaction with another person goes positively or not, the result cannot be any worse than if you just remained passively in your corner!

On the other hand, if you had never approached a person who looked nice, they would undoubtedly have never approached you either and you would probably have never made their acquaintance.

As a matter of fact, this pertains to most of your friends. It is most probably down to the fact that you approached them first that they are your friends now.

Lastly, approaching people gives you the power and freedom to choose those individuals who seem of most interest to you or with whom you think you would get along best. No longer will you be subject to the luck of the draw when it comes to social interactions – it is *you* who makes the choice.

6) LACK OF CONFIDENCE; SHYNESS; PSYCHOLOGICAL BLOCKS

Now that we have grasped what signs of availability are, we shall look into potential explanations for some people's failed attempts to use them.

Amongst the many usual reasons which people give to explain a person's difficulty in fitting in or making friends, mention may be made of those which come up most frequently:

Low self-esteem; family background; a bad experience; cultural differences; shyness; anxiety; fear of rejection; introverted character, and so on.

These are general statements and stereotypes which we hear everywhere unfortunately, be it on people's lips, in personal development books or psychology magazines. There are both true and false elements to these statements.

It is **true** that the task of social integration is made harder and less instinctive due to certain character traits or psychological blocks such as those mentioned above. Indeed, introverted people do tend to have a reputation for their reflective, reclusive temperament. They can feel mentally exhausted when faced with too much social stimuli. Similarly, we should point out that an exaggerated dread of the way people view others can significantly inhibit the social skills of an anxious person who will experience difficulty in keeping up a conversation.

It is **false** because there are many introverted, anxious people with poor self-esteem all over the world, who, despite everything, manage to build friendly relationships and fit into society perfectly well. We all know a highly reserved person in our circle of friends and family who flourishes at work and goes out with his or her friends every weekend. It is a real, indisputable fact that there are a great many people who have a variety of psychological blocks (fear of rejection, hang-ups, traumas, etc.). This certainly makes it harder for them to interact but in no way does it prevent them from forming good, satisfying, friendly relationships.

All in all, whatever the underlying nature of the problems (cultural, familial or psychological), the most crucial thing to grasp is that in the final analysis...

...It is your signs of availability that are "disrupted" when you meet people which risk sending erroneous information to others!

Indeed, this can be seen in the case of a very shy person who feels uncomfortable at a party because of his or her subconscious fear of other people's judgement.

It is precisely all their signs of availability which are affected: *avoidance of eye contact; embarrassed grin; disjointed conversation; hesitant or closed demeanour; stays in their corner, and so forth.*

That is the main reason why some timid, reserved people feel invisible within groups. No one notices that they are there, not because of their personality or looks, but because they do not send sufficiently clear signs of availability to others!

There can be multiple reasons for disruption of our signs of availability specific to each person's background. The table below provides you with clues to find out the causes:

Examples of possible causes	**Watch out for repercussions and incorrect use of your signs of availability when you go out!**
Shyness, anxiety or social phobia	I avoid eye contact and have a tense smile. My conversation is disjointed and I sit in my corner...
Poor self-esteem; lack of confidence	I feel boring and worthless compared with the other guests. I do everything I can to avoid saying unintelligent things. So, I remain silent...
Physical hang-ups	I'm afraid of people seeing that ugly birthmark on my face, so I tense up and often lower my head...
Existential unease	I sulk, I withdraw into myself, I seem to be preoccupied all the time...
Mistrust, traumas	I'm suspicious about people because of old personal traumas. I tend to dig my heels in and be overprotective of myself...
Autism, Asperger's Syndrome	I find eye contact with people hard to bear. I take up funny postures. I always have the same facial expression and live in my own bubble...
A too reflective, serious character	This is the problem with people who are too serious or inflexible: they rarely smile and their closed attitude can be interpreted as signs of unavailability...

This table is not intended to enumerate every single potential difficulty which people might encounter in their interactions with others, as each topic tackled is a unique, complex subject with the advice provided being specific to each theme. The idea of this book is not to reject explanations of a psychological or cultural nature. The table merely aims to draw your attention to the fact that, unbeknownst to you, some of your blocks may lead to your using signs of availability incorrectly and be the reason you have problems fitting in!

 Gaining awareness of this is to realise that you are able to make a change and finally assume the most suitable demeanour in public.

The important thing is to manage to compensate for one's shortcomings and to appear available, either by 'repairing' affected signs of availability or by opting for others.

In the next few chapters, we shall actually see that solutions do exist for surmounting all these various impediments. Problems, such as a lack of self-esteem or a highly introverted character, may be too entrenched and complicated to be resolved definitively. Some are even inherent to the nature of our personality and it is best to learn how to accept oneself and live with them. We shall broach another of the book's fundamental concepts: signs of sociability. This will include coming to understand that our psychological blocks and different complexes do not in any way prevent us from connecting with others, provided that one knows how to make proper use of these signs of sociability.

CHAPTER IV

TEN TYPES OF SIGNS OF SOCIABILITY TO COMMUNICATE SUCCESSFULLY WHEN YOU MEET PEOPLE

1) SIGNS OF SOCIABILITY ARE USED FOR COMMUNICATION

Communication is the capacity of a person to hold a face-to-face interaction throughout the encounter either by conversation or non-verbal interaction.

Every day, you come across many people in the tube, street or at work. However, there are really very few people with whom you do communicate. Indeed, most of the time you display a preoccupied or passive expression, and at work it is even more the case when you are in a business surrounded by a hundred workers, as you cannot say 'hello' and converse with everybody. You are obliged to use your signs of availability to filter your social interactions on a day-to-day basis!

As we have seen in previous chapters, signs of availability are what are used by a person to show him or herself to be available or otherwise, in a particular territory before a real conversation does take place. They are the first stage of an individual's socialisation with their social environment.

By contrast, signs of sociability are what a person uses to conduct a social interaction and connect with someone. It is the time for **dynamic communication**, such as having a conversation; listening; touching people in a friendly manner; making jokes, etc.

Signs of sociability are the second stage of an individual's socialisation during which he or she will interact directly with the other person to create a relationship.

Let us recap on the difference between signs of availability and signs of sociability with the following diagram.

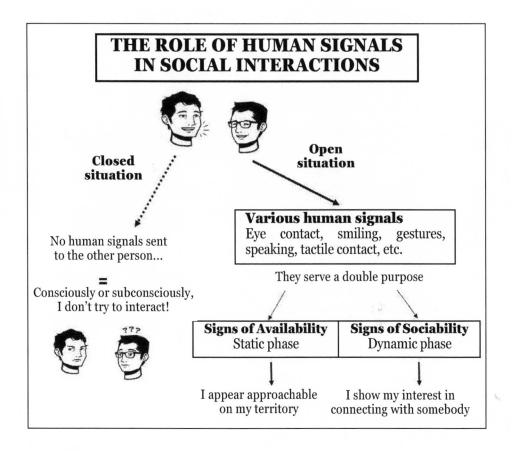

THE ROLE OF HUMAN SIGNALS IN SOCIAL INTERACTIONS

Closed situation

Open situation

No human signals sent to the other person...

=

Consciously or subconsciously, I don't try to interact!

Various human signals
Eye contact, smiling, gestures, speaking, tactile contact, etc.

They serve a double purpose

Signs of Availability Static phase	**Signs of Sociability** Dynamic phase
I appear approachable on my territory	I show my interest in connecting with somebody

We are now going to see what the various signs of sociability are. They are intrinsic to every human being and we shall start by examining them amongst people considered to be the most sociable.

It turns out that they are the ones who know how to use them best in their social communication!

2) HYPERSOCIAL PEOPLE'S SOCIAL COMMUNICATION

The following cannot have escaped anybody's attention: highly sociable people are possessed of that astonishing gift of instinctively attracting others to them when they interact in public.

Here, we suggest a term to designate highly sociable individuals: *hypersocial* people. They enjoy ideal social communication skills which allow them swiftly to create interactions and forge ties with others.

Regardless of how many people are in the room, hypersocial individuals generally have the knack of being accepted by everyone, often within the first few minutes. They do not go unnoticed because they are warm and radiate a kind of social aura. Even the most timid people feel comfortable and enjoy communicating with them.

You are sure to have met hypersocial people already over the course of your life or you know extremely sociable people in your circle of friends and family. How can we explain their success with people? What do we notice in particular about their social behaviour?

The idea here is not to turn yourself into a person you are not, but to grasp the underlying codes of successful social communication in order for you to use them yourself!

Actually, as we shall see, every human being is furnished with a range of signs of sociability, and, quite simply, hypersocial individuals use them more and better than most others.

Amongst the signs of sociability that exist in our human nature, there are ten which are decisive when meeting people and which may play a social attraction role. What are they?

Let us try to understand by looking at the social communication of hypersocial people set out in a table and making comments about each aspect...

No	SIGNS OF SOCIABILITY	Attraction Effect	DECYPHERING: What do hypersocial people do more than others?
1	Eye contact		They have a sincere expression. They look the person they are talking to in the eye more often than most people do.
2	Smiling		They have a winning smile. They are always beaming. Even on the telephone, you can hear them smiling.
3	Conversation		Their conversation is animated. They know how to keep a chat going, to talk about themselves, the rain or fine weather, whilst retaining your attention.
4	Open body language		They use gestures to express themselves. They touch the person they are talking to more than most people would: long and friendly handshake, taps on the shoulder, warm physical contact, etc.
5	Interest in others; listening		They do not limit themselves to speaking but are also good listeners. They ask questions and take a genuine interest in people.
6	Paying someone a sincere compliment		They pay personalised compliments to show their interest in the people they meet, without being unctuous.
7	Appearing to be conciliatory with others		Whilst being assertive, they seek consensus rather than opposition. This can be seen in many signs of approval, such as smiling, agreement, and nodding of the head.
8	Good mood or sense of humour		They have a positive, enthusiastic mindset. They enjoy joking around and telling nice, amusing little stories to create a good atmosphere.
9	Expressing one's gratitude to others		They externalise their positive feelings towards people when they like them, showing appreciation, friendship and expressing affection.
10	Taking the initiative; inviting others		They do not remain passive but are enterprising at the very least, making friendly advances, suggestions, invitations and offers to go out.

These are universal traits which everyone can notice in the sociable people they have met over their lifetime!

From this diagram, we can see that there are ten types of signs of sociability which everyone can use to their advantage, simply in order to show themselves as being sociable.

"Look at the other person, listen to them, smile at them, take an interest in them – for me, being a human being starts there" as Sister Emmanuelle would say.

Every time you meet a person who seems genial, ponder to yourself what their signs of sociability are. There are one or more they have used subconsciously which have **made you find them likeable**.

The defining feature of hypersocial people is precisely that they do have a skill for bringing together most of these signs of sociability. That is where their incredible power of social magnetism comes from.

However, as humans, we are not compelled to learn how to master all of this at once so as to communicate with others and make friends. As we shall see, it is sufficient to know how to use appropriate signs of sociability; those that are in keeping with our personality.

Comments on Using the Table:

♦ In human nature, there are sure to be other signs of sociability which help everyone appear sociable to another person. However, for the sake of clarity and overall consistency, we have decided to select the ten principal ones which will serve as 'markers', allowing the reader to pick them out easily.

♦ Obviously, the idea is not to interpret each of the table's components in a sequential fashion, but to comprehend it in the following way: smiling or using friendly physical gestures towards the other person can make you more attractive socially.

♦ By contrast, constantly avoiding eye contact or always being at variance may give rise to a feeling of unease or rejection in the other person. Nevertheless, later on we shall see that some types of awkward behaviour are not unacceptable if they are correctly compensated for with other signs of sociability!

♦ The ten signs of sociability do not all have the same value and importance. Paying compliments and having a sense of humour are certainly appealing factors but they too are not indispensable in connecting with others. However, conversation and eye contact do seem to be the most decisive universal criteria which enable an interaction to have a positive outcome, even though not having these characteristics can be overcome if positive compensation is used, as we shall come to see later on.

WHAT ABOUT SIGNS OF SOCIABILITY AMONGST ANIMALS?

As animals cannot communicate with words, their signs of sociability are chiefly of two types: **physical contact** and **vocalisations**.

For example, many mammals (dogs, lions, zebra, monkeys) show affection by stroking or rubbing against each other, and mutually delousing and sniffing one another. Body contact signifies a social bond between them.

Other animals (macaques, dolphins, birds) use vocal sounds and special cries to communicate, gather in groups or help each other when faced with a threat.

3) THE TABLE OF TEN SIGNS OF SOCIABILITY

Before going any further, and so that things are perfectly clear, let us summarise these concepts in the following new diagram...

THE TEN TYPES OF SIGNS OF SOCIABILITY

During a friendly chat...

Am I showing the other person signs of sociability?

There are ten which exist in human nature. They are used to show that you are willing and glad to interact with the other person:

1) I look them in the eye
2) I smile
3) I make conversation
4) I make friendly physical contact with them
5) I take an interest in them; I listen to them
6) I pay them a sincere compliment
7) I know how to be conciliatory
8) I joke with them
9) I express my appreciation
10) I take the initiative; I invite them

"Being sociable doesn't just mean talking but knowing how to show one's other signs of sociability."

Proper comprehension of the Table of the Ten Signs of Sociability is of fundamental importance and serves as a reference for the rest of the book. Indeed, thanks to this, you will come to understand the following, amongst other things:

- Why some introverted or extremely reserved people manage to thrive in their social relations despite everything.

- Why some people succeed in making friends in spite of profound psychological blocks, such as a lack of self-confidence, a fear of rejection, and anxiety.

- Why some people manage to form relationships and are appreciated by others despite yet greater disabilities, such as social phobia, Asperger's Syndrome and motor impairments.

All the cases mentioned do really exist and you will definitely have come across some of them during your life. Introverted or shy people and dropouts who have many friends and who are able to communicate with people – yes, such individuals do exist! Yet, seeing that you were undoubtedly impressed with their social communication when you met them, never for a moment will you have had an inkling that deep down they were hugely withdrawn and had learnt to fit into society through their experiences.

You will have grasped from the Ten Signs of Sociability Table that whatever your personality or individual blocks, you will always have room for manoeuvre in your encounters because of your social communication.

Bear in mind that these Ten Signs of Sociability are **natural components of social attraction**. They help "attract" like magnets.

For instance, there are people who are not very talkative but, because they are able to compensate for their reserved character with other strong signs of sociability, such as their communicative smile, empathy or gestural communication, they do seem to be sociable and hospitable in other people's estimation. All in all, they fit in well with groups.

We shall now look at three real-life stories for the purposes of illustrating these statements and gaining a proper understanding of the subjects at hand. In our life, we have all come across such types of personality. These particular ones have succeeded in forming relationships by using their various signs of sociability!

For greater clarity, here is an explanation of the legend indicating the meaning of each icon in the Ten Signs of Sociability Tables:

Icon	Legend
😊⚡🧲	**Social Attraction Effect:** This means that it is one of your inherent qualities; it is part of your social communication which people might especially appreciate!
😞✗🧲	**The Awkwardness or Social Repulsion Effect:** This means that it is one of your weaknesses; it is part of your social communication which might make people feel uncomfortable or bring about rejection.
	Blank: Of little significance. You either normally use this component of social communication or you rarely use it.

In the tables below, some of the lines have deliberately been left empty with no icon, primarily with a view to highlighting the principal strengths and weaknesses of the social communication of each person studied.

FIRST REAL-LIFE EXAMPLE:

Case study of Larry, 36 years old, webmaster, extremely reserved

Larry does not talk a lot at work. He often speaks in short sentences and avoids long monologues. He is fairly retiring and does not like to talk about himself. He prefers to ask other people questions to get them to talk about themselves. His colleagues do not hear from him much.

However, being able to make conversation seems to be the most fundamentally important social skill in order to interact with others. Nonetheless, this does not prevent Larry from being liked by his colleagues and integrating into the team perfectly. How is this possible? Let us try and understand the reasons for his social success thanks to the Ten Signs of Sociability Table.

No	SIGNS OF SOCIABILITY	Attraction Effect	COMMENTS:
1	Eye contact		
2	Smiling	☺ ⚡ 🧲	This is his best attribute. Larry has a winning smile. He often smiles and does so whenever his colleagues come over to chat with him.
3	Conversation	☹ ✗ 🧲	Larry is not very talkative. This is his main drawback and it is not exactly a small one when it comes to trying to fit in! His replies are cursory. He makes do with a few inconsequential remarks during a conversation or he asks questions to get other people to do the talking.
4	Open body language		
5	Interest in others; listening		
6	Paying a sincere compliment	☹ ✗ 🧲	Larry does not show his feelings and avoids revealing anything about himself. Furthermore, he does not pay compliments to others precisely because of this excessive reticence.
7	Appearing to be conciliatory	☺ ⚡ 🧲	Larry knows how to fit in with others. His smile of approval, the nodding of his head and his kind attentiveness show that he is conciliatory and makes himself available.
8	Good mood or sense of humour	☺ ⚡ 🧲	He does not joke around very much and never tells funny stories. However, he does laugh with his colleagues when they are joking amongst themselves. His winning smile gives the impression that he is always in a good mood.
9	Expressing one's gratitude to others		
10	Taking the initiative; inviting others	☺ ⚡ 🧲	When his colleagues suggest that he joins them for a friendly drink, Larry accepts and takes an active part in company life. He always turns up when invited and takes the initiative, for example, by bringing croissants to his colleagues in the morning.

<u>Conclusion</u>:

Although Larry is not talkative and is a reticent type of person, he fits in well with the team. Being sociable does not necessarily mean being voluble all the time. His winning smile is a plus point and makes him appear amiable. He respects social codes and is conciliatory. He does not remain passive – he makes himself available to others by taking part in company life, accepting invitations to drinks and occasionally taking the initiative.

Ultimately, Larry is comfortable with his personality and constantly displays signs of sociability. This allows him to be accepted by his colleagues who, over time, have got used to his highly reserved character. Nobody criticises him for it. Larry's case is not exceptional and reflects the position of millions of introverted and happy employees throughout the world. Think about it – you surely have come across people like him in businesses where you have worked!

<u>SECOND REAL-LIFE EXAMPLE</u>:

Case study of Laura, 25 years old, economics student, social anxiety

Laura has always been a timid person. She has a thoughtful, hypersensitive personality. She lacks self-confidence and easily becomes stressed by exams or having to make oral presentations. Laura does not go out a lot at the weekend, preferring to devote her time to study or her love of the piano. At university, even though she gets distressed in group situations, she forces herself to approach her colleagues and take part in discussions.

The method which she has found to overcome her anxiety is to be inquisitive and take a genuine interest in others. This spurs her on to get to know people. Let us take a look at the Ten Signs of Sociability Table for Laura and see, for instance, which ones she uses to connect with people.

No	SIGNS OF SOCIABILITY	Attraction Effect	COMMENTS:
1	Eye contact		
2	Smiling		
3	Conversation		Even though Laura is a reserved person, she does at least know how to hold a conversation. She is capable of expressing what she is thinking about and adapting to discussion topics.
4	Open body language	☹ ✗ 🧲	Most of the time, she assumes a type of posture which at first sight looks closed and defensive. She becomes more comfortable as the conversation progresses.
5	Interest in others; listening	☺ ⚡ 🧲	Her sensitivity is a plus point and means she can be empathetic towards people. She tries to get to know them and asks questions. She takes a genuine interest in others.
6	Paying a sincere compliment	☺ ⚡ 🧲	When Laura notices a positive attribute in the person to whom she is talking, she is the kind of person to make a nice remark about it because she likes pleasing others.
7	Appearing to be conciliatory		
8	Good mood or sense of humour	☹ ✗ 🧲	Her friends think she is too serious. Laura is contemplative and dreamy. She prefers deep conversations to lightweight banter but that does not stop her from joking around with her pals from time to time.
9	Expressing one's gratitude to others	☺ ⚡ 🧲	Despite Laura's solitary character, she has benevolent qualities. She is able to express her gratitude to her friends; to be altruistic; and externalise her positive feelings towards those she likes, something which is vital in forming relationships.
10	Taking the initiative; inviting others	☺ ⚡ 🧲	Laura makes the first move in approaching others to initiate conversation. When it comes to friendship, she prefers quality over quantity. At university, she has one or two friends to whom she often extends friendly invitations to go and eat out together.

<u>Conclusion:</u>

At university, in spite of Laura's social anxiety, she forces herself to approach other students and have lunch with them. Every time, she becomes afraid, she says the following phrases to herself, repeating them like a magic formula:

"Who are these people really behind their façade? What can they do for me and what can I do for them?"

Although Laura is serious and a homebody, the important thing is that she knows how to make use of her signs of sociability when she meets people she takes to by externalising her feelings of affability: friendly advances, sincere compliments, words of appreciation. Other people receive her signs of sociability and can reciprocate, ultimately enabling her to connect with others.

<u>THIRD REAL-LIFE EXAMPLE</u>:

Case study of Lucy, 42 years old, marketing director,
hard to please when it comes to relationships

Lucy feels comfortable around people and fits in with a group fairly quickly. She is chatty and enthusiastic and likes giving her opinion on all sorts of subjects, sometimes to the point of monopolising the conversation. At work, she commands her colleagues' respect. Lucy uses her hands when talking and puts her ideas across accompanied by expressive gestures. She exudes confidence and is able to win people's attention.

However, when the weekend comes round, she often finds herself at home, alone. She is saddened not to have a few close friends in whom she can confide. How can we explain the fact that, despite her having an extroverted character, she has difficulties in forming relationships? Let us try and understand the reasons why, using the Ten Signs of Sociability Table.

No	SIGNS OF SOCIABILITY	Attraction Effect	COMMENTS:
1	Eye Contact		
2	Smiling	☺ ⚡ 🧲	Lucy smiles easily. She is generally eager and has self-confidence.
3	Conversation	☺ ⚡ 🧲	Lucy is chatty and keen on many topics. She is used to taking a central role in conversations with others, whether with the family or at work.
4	Open body language	☺ ⚡ 🧲	Lucy communicates a great deal with her hands. This is one of her great assets because her gestural ability attracts people's attention at meetings and luncheons.
5	Interest in others; listening	☹ ✖ 🧲	As much as she might be willing to talk to everyone, when it comes to having more personal interactions, she clams up. She hardly listens and does not have time for people who are not like her, such as those who have opposing political beliefs or come from a cultural background far removed from hers.
6	Paying a sincere compliment		
7	Appearing to be conciliatory		
8	Good mood or sense of humour		
9	Expressing one's gratitude to others		
10	Taking the initiative; inviting others	☹ ✖ 🧲	Lucy does not make friendly advances to others and often finds an excuse to turn down invitations. This is due to her lack of open-mindedness because as soon as Lucy senses that the other person brings her no benefit, she does not try to take the relationship any further. As a result, she has a passive stance with her acquaintances.

Conclusion:

On the face of things, Lucy is a sociable woman. She is proficient in her social communication both verbal (conversation) and non-verbal (smiling, gestures). This explains why she successfully manages all her social interaction. What is more, she is usually in an enthusiastic mood and radiates confidence. She attracts people socially straightaway. In the Table, this entire section of her social communication is depicted above by positive magnets.

However, her propensity for ignoring friendly advances and only favouring a single category of people because of her prejudices, quite simply prevents her from making friends! In this example, Lucy's particular case highlights the importance of a universal factor which is essential for forming friendly ties: taking practical initiatives. In the same way as the two previous stories, these are examples of personalities which exist in everyday life and which you will have encountered during your life.

NOW, IT IS YOUR TURN TO EXAMINE
YOUR OWN SOCIAL COMMUNICATION:

Your signs of sociability must be in keeping with your personality!

You will now understand the principle of how the Ten Signs of Sociability Table works. Using the three previous examples, you will be able to complete your own using the empty chart shown on the next page. The Table encourages you to reflect on what the real assets and drawbacks are of your social communication. Ultimately, this will help you adopt the appropriate social behaviour when you interact with others.

Here following are a few reminders of the basic principles so that you can use the Table correctly:

- **Every human has to his name a whole collection of action methods to interact successfully with his or her fellow human beings. We will call this an Armoury of Signs of Sociability.**

- **We have enumerated ten which exist in human nature. The Ten Signs of Sociability are biological factors of social attraction.**

- Being sociable does not necessarily mean being someone who is talkative or extroverted but really denotes the following: showing signs of sociability to others.
  If one of your signs of sociability is lacking, simply go for another type – you will always have leeway.

- To be in harmony with other people, search in your Armoury of Signs of Sociability for those Signs which are in keeping with your personality, and concentrate on them when you meet people.

Practical Examples:

- If, in spite of your shyness or social anxiety, you feel deep down that you do have an excellent sense of humour and an ability to make fun of things, then, in your relationships, use smiling (*No. 2*) and a sense of humour (*No. 8*) from the list of the Ten Signs of Sociability.

- If, on the other hand, you have a rather serious or melancholic character, but you do know that you are also someone who is sensitive and affective, then opt for listening and empathy (*No. 5*) or expressing one's gratitude to others (*No. 10*) to connect with people.

- Body language (gestures, physical contact) is an integral part of social communication. If you are content with your body and like to speak whilst using gestures (*No. 4*), then make use of them in your social interactions. There are indeed extremely reserved people who do not communicate a lot verbally, but the mere fact that they are very expressive with their gestures gives them the appearance of someone who is open and confident.

- If one of your signs of sociability is lacking due to a noticeable impediment or disability, sometimes trying too hard is of no use. The most important thing is to compensate in another way through better mastery of other signs of sociability which you can employ as social attraction mechanisms. As such, some autistic people, who have extreme difficulty in holding eye contact with the person to whom they are talking and decoding facial expressions, manage to integrate into society by developing other social aptitudes, such as conversation (*No 3*), appearing to be conciliatory (*No. 7*) or taking the initiative (*No. 9*).

Photocopy the Ten Signs of Sociability Table and fill it in...

No	SIGNS OF SOCIABILITY	Attraction Effect	YOUR COMMENTS:
1	Eye contact		
2	Smiling		
3	Conversation		
4	Open body language		
5	Interest in others; listening		
6	Paying a sincere compliment		
7	Appearing to be conciliatory		
8	Good mood or sense of humour		
9	Expressing one's gratitude to others		
10	Taking the initiative; inviting others		

REMEMBER! At the end of the book, you will find practical, clear and detailed **info sheets** which are grouped according to theme, to help you understand and know how to use each one of the Ten Signs of Sociability when meeting people. Consult the info sheets if you want to get some ideas and practical examples to help you conduct a conversation, pay a sincere compliment, take the initiative with others, and so on.

CHAPTER V

GENERAL SUMMARY:

THE THREE UNIVERSAL STAGES TO GO THROUGH TO AVOID MISSING OUT ON INTERACTING WITH PEOPLE

1) APPROACHING PEOPLE, COMMUNICATING, TAKING THE INITIATIVE

In the chapter dealing with signs of availability, we have seen that the principal factor in getting to meet someone was the act of approaching them.

Likewise, in the previous chapter, we have seen that there are various ways of communicating with another person, including talking, smiling, paying a compliment, being expressive with gestures, and so forth.

With the various examples examined, we nevertheless observed that the most decisive factor in connecting with people was taking practical initiatives.

In an interaction, there are always **interruptions**, gaps, pauses, periods of silence; or even when you have stopped interacting with a person because they have said goodbye to you!

Some people who find it very hard to interact (chatting, holding eye contact) manage to connect with people despite everything because they do know how to look active during these interruptions. What is their secret? They simply take the initiative.

> Taking practical initiatives means helping an interaction with a person progress constantly, whether it is in a discussion or a relationship, and not letting it suddenly fizzle out!

For instance, in a chat with one of your pals, take the initiative. For example:

Wake up the discussion during moments of silence; propose an activity if the conversation peters out; make friendly advances; suggest extending the get-together in a convivial meeting place so that you can get to know them better, and so on.

For instance, aside from face-to-face meetings or at home, take the initiative:

Send your pal messages to find out how they are; phone them; suggest meeting up; invite them round, etc.

In the end, whatever blunder you might make in your social communication, approaching people, communicating and taking the initiative remain the three essential stages if you want to succeed in forming a true bond.

When you meet someone for the first time, there is a logical order to follow to ensure that a successful interaction ensues in all circumstances:

1- I APPROACH PEOPLE

2- I COMMUNICATE (verbal and non-verbal)

3- I TAKE PRACTICAL INITIATIVES

When you go out, always keep in mind these three rules which will help you stay active during your interactions. If you do not manage to form a simple friendly relationship, ask yourself these questions: *"Did I approach anyone?" "Did I communicate enough with the person I was talking to?" "Did I take practical initiatives?"*

X I don't approach people		▶ Then, quite simply nothing will happen!
X I don't communicate		▶ The person you are talking to might feel uncomfortable…
X I don't take the initiative		▶ You are preventing a friendly relationship from forming.

Communication is the capacity of a person to hold a face-to-face interaction throughout the encounter, either by conversation or non-verbal interaction.

Remember that you have a variety of potential signs of sociability to communicate with another person in a consistent, harmonious way. Employ those signs which are in line with your personality.

Of course, you have every right to be inept when communicating with others! However, remaining passive with people is something you cannot allow yourself to do – therein lies the difference!

2) THE RULE OF THE THREE UNIVERSAL STAGES

Here is a recap in diagram format to aid proper comprehension...

DASHBOARD OF THE THREE STAGES OF CONNECTING WITH PEOPLE

To sum up...
Here's what you should do
when meeting people

1) MAKE THE APPROACH

2) COMMUNICATE — I look at them; I speak; I smile; I listen or I pay a compliment, etc.

3) TAKE THE INITIATIVE

> I DON'T STAY PASSIVE
> DURING INTERRUPTIONS!
> - I reinvigorate the conversation;
>   I start it up again during
>   periods of silence
> - I propose an activity
> - I make friendly advances
> - I suggest things; I invite people

These three stages are universal insofar as they work everywhere, in everyday life and even on the Internet! Indeed, we might find it surprising that many shy, socially phobic or autistic people have no trouble in forming friendly relationships within only a few weeks on the Internet; whereas, in their daily lives, they sometimes cannot even bring themselves to approach strangers.

You will have guessed what the difference is – in real life, they do not comply with those three fundamental rules (approaching people, communicating, and taking the initiative) because they are afraid. They dare not do the slightest thing in public, or they are simply too hesitant with others.

By contrast, any hurdles are greatly diminished on the Internet, forums or social networks. These individuals are in their comfort zone – they appear to be more open; they approach others by sending Private Messages; joining online chat; and making friendly advances. They succeed in connecting with other Internet users and all because in that setting they do tick the three boxes: making the approach; communicating, and taking the initiative!

Moreover, generally speaking, the rules of the social game also apply to the Internet. If you do not interact with anybody, logically, nothing will happen. The more you interact with people, the more opportunities you create to meet people or to strengthen an existing tie.

On discussion forums and Facebook, if you take a genuine interest in a person and interact with them often, then there is a good chance that they will take a reciprocal interest in you.

Many Internet users manage to connect with people because they made the first move and showed their interest in someone by posting on their timeline, making comments on their humorous posts, writing messages of sympathy or support, and so on. And, just like in real life, people will react to your advances, get curious, and seek to interact with you via your messages or by showing their appreciation.

 WHAT ABOUT SOCIAL CODES ON THE INTERNET?

This works on Skype, WhatsApp, social networks and forums too… Here, we can have fun making parallels to get a clearer picture!

Writing a message to a stranger; adding a friend = *making the approach*
Chatting online = *communicating*
Inviting someone to play or go out = *taking the initiative*

Sending a 'poke' (Facebook) = *making a friendly advance*
Unavailable, busy (Skype) = *signs of unavailability*
Smileys = *signs of sociability to show a smile or a token of gratitude*

CHAPTER VI

PSYCHODIVERSITY:

ACCEPTING ONE'S INDIVIDUALITY; FINDING ONE'S PLACE AMONGST OTHERS

1) INTROVERSION; SHYNESS

Knowing who you are and how you go about things is also essential if you want to fit in. Many shy or introverted people are troubled by their individuality; whereas, they should actually be learning how to come to terms with their nature. People often confuse the terms 'shyness' and 'introversion', words which do not have quite the same meanings. Although both words are similar, they are in fact distinct from one another – an introvert is not necessarily shy. This Chapter sets out to clarify various ideas and avoid mixing things up!

♦ **Shyness:** to most people, this term is synonymous with a lack of confidence. From a psychological perspective, it is a form of hypersensitivity to the fear of being judged by others. This occurs to such an extent amongst shy individuals that it erodes their means of social communication, including avoidance of eye contact; tense body language; disjointed conversation, and so on.

♦ **Introversion:**[7] this term designates a personality trait associated with the mind's "processing depth." In a social situation, introverted individuals are not fundamentally anxious but seek more depth in conversations, and they are more contemplative and stimulated by solitary rather than group activities.

For example, when a **shy person** arrives at a meeting room, they will be highly sensitive to other people's judgement. It is as if they felt they were being observed and were the central focus of people's attention. Such a person will feel intense discomfort when they are given the opportunity of speaking in public. Imagine now that there is a buffet at the end of the meeting. That timid person will not necessarily feel comfortable approaching others or taking part in the group ambience for fear of not knowing what to say.

Conversely, social situations are not anxiety-provoking factors for an introverted person. That is the difference between shyness and introversion. An **introverted person** arriving at a meeting room will not automatically feel anxiety on interacting with others or speaking publicly. Where a shy person can only manage to make feeble, erratic conversation due to their fear of how they are perceived by others, the introvert is able to feel at ease and have good control of his or her social communication.

Introversion is a psychological temperament; a character trait associated with the mind's processing depth.

Therefore, perhaps most of the reserved people who you know in your life are not shy but just introverted, or potentially both. Amongst the most frequent signs which describe introverted people, we may note the following:

- They think more before speaking.
- They are more comfortable having conversations in small groups rather than large ones.
- In discussions, they look more for depth than the mere exchange of trivialities.
- They prefer a peaceful environment to noisy settings.

- Social activities tend to exhaust their energy whereas solitary activities help them recharge their batteries, such as reading, walking, working on the computer, etc.

- They like to have control of situations and have a low tolerance for the unforeseen, such as unexpected telephone calls or impromptu parties.
- They withdraw into themselves when they feel their energy has been depleted and prefer to retreat rather than forcing themselves into talking.

Introverts are more contemplative by virtue of the different way their mind works. They feel events with the full intensity of their inwardness. This is in contrast to extroverts who "think out loud" and are accordingly more lively and instinctive in their relations with others and the world. They feel events with the full intensity of the present moment, as is presented to them by unfiltered events.

It is said that extroverts draw their energy from contact with others and social activities, whilst introverts recharge their batteries from solitary activities.

The ideals and values advocated by our modern society – at least in the West as opposed to Asia – favour the cult of extroversion: communication, spontaneity, leadership, social networks, having a cool, fun attitude, and so on. Extroversion is perceived as the ideal to pursue, whereas introversion has negative connotations described by such adjectives as shy, solitary and asocial. As a consequence, this leads to a feeling of disquiet in every person who does not deem themselves as belonging to the norm. Hence, this is also a societal problem.

Moreover, in our daily lives, we feel as if we are surrounded only by extroverted people. We focus solely on them because we are impressed primarily by their attributes, conversation and positive energy. Also, we do not notice introverted people because some of them are playing the role of extrovert to fit in with society.

In truth, 30% to 40% of the population are estimated to be introverted.[8] So, being a reserved person who does not feel the need to talk all the time is not an anomaly!

Let us simply remember that introversion relates to a form of the mind's processing depth; a psychic reaction orientated inwardly rather than outwardly. Thus, it follows that the qualities of introverts lie in their character traits, such as attentiveness, empathy, composure, analysis, depth, creativity, etc.

In society, it is usual to fit in with people and to be at least a little bit sociable, otherwise one risks being excluded from the group. However, fitting in does not mean getting rid of one's introversion but instead means **having suitable social communication** with others!

In order to lead a happy, thriving life, the main thing is to find a harmonious balance between the demands relating to life in society (work, the group, conversations) and the needs associated with your personality (quiet, seeking depth, the need to withdraw).

It is possible to reconcile both. On the next page, there are a few tips which will help towards this end. This advice applies to every person who finds social contact to be an ordeal...

A FEW TIPS FOR THE INTROVERT
TO MAKE EVERYDAY LIFE EASIER

♦ Accept the fact that introversion is an integral part of your nature:
Introversion is not an illness. Our modern society and the media put more of an emphasis on values relating to extroversion (communication, laughing, cooperation, etc.), which engenders a sense of unease in the introvert who feels different when he or she is in fact normal!

♦ Learn how to socialise in your own way:
Choose the times when you want to socialise instead of forcing yourself to play a role all the time.
When you go out in a group, it may happen that you feel exhausted after having chatted for a while. You are entitled to be more reserved or quiet. If you get stuck, the main thing is to go for available social communication (A.S.C.), as we shall see later on.

♦ List five conversational topics you feel strongly about:
An introverted person can find speaking about trivialities takes quite an effort. So, it is easier to have some favourite conversational topics up your sleeve to liven things up when you meet people. Pinpoint them. In this way, you will find that speaking without pushing yourself comes more naturally to you.

♦ Recovering your energy through solitary activities:
Following intense social activity, the introvert feels the need to withdraw, to recharge his or her batteries through solitary activities. This is normal and healthy. Allow yourself micro-breaks throughout your day – re-energise yourself in the countryside, by walking, reading or doing a creative activity.

♦ Focus on friendly ties with the right people:
In society, one has to fit in and be open to everybody. However, in private, you have the freedom to choose. Concentrate on quality rather than quantity in your relationships: genuine discussions, going out in a small group and being in the company of people with whom you can form a meaningful, friendly relationship.

2) FEAR OF OTHER PEOPLE'S PERCEPTION = A HYPERSENSITIVE IAS

As we have seen, some introverted individuals do not worry in the least about other people's perception of them.

The individuals who do suffer from this, who are referred to as shy, are those who are extremely sensitive to other people's judgement. In social situations (speaking in public, walking in the street, talking to a stranger), they may have the unpleasant feeling of being watched or judged. As soon as others pay attention to them, uneasiness prevails and their social communication (eye contact, conversation and gestures) is severely affected or hampered, depending on circumstances.

For example, at school, for fear of being judged, a shy pupil may suddenly stop writing in his exercise book when the teacher comes down his aisle and watches him taking notes. He may experience anxiety when he is waiting for the teacher to say his name at the calling of the register or during oral tests. Oral presentations in front of the class represent the very peak of dread for a pathologically shy person.

What one must understand is that the fear of other people's perception is a natural, universal, psychological mechanism. Every human being on Earth is obviously sensitive to other's people's judgement. An individual who is totally insensitive to what other people think of him or her would commit reprehensible, deviant acts – he or she would be uncontrollable; would walk around naked in public; belch at dinner; and constantly interrupt people when they were talking! Society would operate chaotically and no social interaction would be possible or coherent.

Therefore, every human being has to be equipped with an innate sensitivity mechanism in relation to other people's perception in order to facilitate interaction with his or her fellow human beings. This is required for group cohesion and compliance with society's norms. We are all sensitive to the judgement of others in varying degrees and the feeling of embarrassment or shame is a natural emotion which reminds us of limits not to be overstepped.

Consequently, fear of other people's judgement is a psychological mechanism which plays a regulatory role in human interactions and which we shall call the Internal Alarm System[9] (IAS)

With shy or anxious people, the problem is that this internal biological alarm system is disturbed. As a result, such individuals are hypersensitive to other people's judgement of them. The IAS is constantly in turmoil and easily triggered. This is an emotional hyper-reactivity comparable to an allergic reaction, which is an immune hyper-reactivity to a given allergen. It works in the same way. The brain detects a danger and reacts accordingly. This is a malfunction of the threat detector. The IAS can be measured on a scale of 1 to 10.

Here is an example of what this looks like in real life: At the beginning of the school term, a shy person arrives late and enters the classroom. They suddenly find the other pupils' attention is focused on them – their IAS will cut in at a very high rate (8/10). Their heart rate increases; they avoid eye contact; and their movements are uncertain. They hurry over to sit on the last bench at the back of the room. When the teacher asks them to do a brief oral test, the pupil panics; their IAS reacts again and it takes them a lot of effort just to get the words out because of their emotional state. The pupil feels awkward and does not know what to say…

However, back home with their family at the end of the day, they will cease to be shy. They will be voluble at the dinner table, chatting without holding back. Their IAS will be at normal level (0/10) because they are in a familiar situation.

This explains why gradual exposure, together with working on the limiting beliefs you have, are recognised as the best remedy for overcoming problems of shyness and anxiety. This consists of steadily confronting dreaded social situations so that fear decreases with familiarity. It is the same principle of desensitisation as with allergies. In this instance, the aim is to reduce the sensitivity of the IAS

As long as one tries to avoid a situation (for example, speaking in front of the class), our IAS associated with this experience will linger at around the 8/10 mark, causing emotional reactions, such as 'stage fright' and trembling of the hands. However, when these situations are faced in a sensible, gradual way by the pupil altering his or her beliefs and repeating the action regularly, they will have a good chance of reducing their IAS to 4/10 over a period of weeks.

Of course, depending on the person's temperament, and his or her capacity for resilience, fear can never be totally eradicated. Reactions of anxiety may continue to arise at any time and this is normal. The main thing is to learn how to control our IAS in order for us not to find it a struggle to accomplish our everyday tasks.

LET'S RECAP:

OTHER PEOPLE'S PERCEPTION = ALARM!

Fear of other people's judgement is a normal, universal psychological mechanism, inherent to every human.

♦ **Shyness** is an excessive form of sensitivity to other people's assessment and judgement.
Lack of self-confidence, reserve, and avoidance are consequences of a disturbed IAS and behavioural conditioning over the years.

♦ **Social anxiety or social phobia** is a debilitating, extreme form of sensitivity to the judgement of others, resulting from an abnormal hyper-reactivity of the IAS.
This may cause extreme cases of physical symptoms in the person (sweats, shaking, panic attacks) and prevent them from going out to take the tube or go shopping.

Cognitive behavioural therapy – CBT (i.e., techniques to help one's cognition together with gradual exposure) is the best known and recommended solution to date.

These new definitions make it possible to have a better grasp of the phenomenon of shyness and social anxiety from a biological perspective.

Today, the question of "nature *versus* nurture" is an outmoded debate. Scientific research generally concurs that shyness and social phobia derive from a combination of nature and nurture. We cannot discard the importance that environment has, nor can we reject the decisive character of innate nature.

According to Jerome Kagan, Professor of Psychology at Harvard University, genes play their role too.[10] He has studied and monitored hundreds of children and babies over several years from their birth to adolescence. He has noted down a multitude of criteria in his records, including: their reaction to strangers or unfamiliar toys; frequency of crying; number of gesticulations; variations in heartbeat; intensity of eye contact, etc. He has noticed that 10 to 15% of children are "high-reactive" and are born with signs of inhibition. When they reach adulthood, most are shyer and more anxious than average, whilst those who are "low-reactive" fit into society better and have more self-confidence when faced with new situations.

He concludes that predispositions in temperament exist due to the amygdala in the brain. People whose amygdala is sensitive become more agitated when faced with unusual stimuli, such as stressful social situations and encounters with strangers.

We may speculate that an internal alarm system specific to social signals exists within the amygdala and that this is biologically disturbed in shy and anxious people.

When such people become aware of a human presence or its appraising eye, all their senses are 'on the lookout'. They feel as if they are being watched; they brood; they anticipate… Their body responds physiologically with a faster heartbeat and increased release of cortisol, the stress hormone. With experience, some timid people manage to curb their fear and thus diminish the IAS's physiological responses. This proves that shyness can be remedied by practising techniques on oneself.

Moreover, we should take note of the particular case of people suffering from Williams Syndrome,[11] where the IAS's process appears to be reversed. This rare illness is caused by a genetic alteration of chromosome 7 and typified by heart defects; mental retardation; and characteristic "elf-like" features. People with Williams Syndrome have a face which looks like an elf or imp. However, they are known for their abnormally effusive behaviour more than anything! They are often cheerful and tactile with others, loquacious, smiling and humming tunes.

It is as if their IAS had been disturbed in the opposite direction – an absence of hyper-reactivity to the fear of others. Children suffering from Williams Syndrome do not mistrust strangers when they meet them. They are very forward, approaching people spontaneously and quickly putting their trust in them. They talk to the bus driver as they would to their best friend, something which is cause for worry for their parents who are compelled to instil caution in them.

Ultimately, from these cases we see that human nature is complex and that there is a diversity of psychological profiles. Some of these demonstrate natural ease in social interactions and some exhibit difficulty and more inhibited behaviour.

SOME TIPS TO OVERCOME THE FEAR OF OTHER PEOPLE'S PERCEPTION OF YOU

♦ **First, be aware that judging people is part of human nature:**
Being afraid of other people's perception of you is a universal psychological mechanism. You must accept the concept that the people you meet might look at you and judge you – that is normal. You too will tend to observe people and make hasty judgements; perhaps even more so than they do?

♦ **Put things into perspective – admit that one can be fallible:**
Nobody's perfect! Mistakes are part of communication. You too will have seen people making blunders on a number of occasions (faltering voice, unease, forgetfulness, etc.) and yet, you forgave them. Indeed, these are things which humans do.

♦ **Remember that other people are far too busy to judge us:**
When you are with people, tell yourself that their attention is taken up by dozens of things (the setting, sounds, your words, their own thoughts, and so on). The reality is that people do not pay attention to details or your slip-ups. Even if they do notice, once they get back home and immerse themselves in their daily routine, they will forget all about them as quick as can be!

♦ **Do not 'think' – follow your impulse straightaway:**
We all have spur-of-the-moment impulses; spontaneous things to say which we dare not for fear of other people's judgement. If we think too much or are too much in control, we risk saying nothing at all or repeating banal phrases. In this instance, the idea is to be in accord with oneself: I have a thought to convey at a given moment; I follow my impulse; and I take action through my words!

♦ **Tell yourself that shyness and anxiety diminish with practice:**
It is normal in specific first-time situations (e.g., taking acting lessons) for you to be in a state of panic and find it hard to control your emotions (IAS = at maximum). It is physiological. Your brain

---

interprets this circumstance as a threat. However, with time, once you have familiarised yourself with your environment, your IAS level can only go down and you will feel more comfortable as the weeks pass. The idea is not to eliminate your anxiety but simply to keep it in check.

3) PSYCHODIVERSITY: WE ALL OPERATE IN A DIFFERENT WAY

Introverted, socially phobic, hypersensitive, intellectually gifted, and so forth… We see these terms appearing in the media and on the Internet more and more. Yes, these psychological concepts have been in vogue for a number of decades and many books have already been written on these topics. You can easily become overwhelmed with all these notions and some people prefer not to be categorised with labels!

Nevertheless, the fact that these terms are overused in the media should not allow us to overlook **the reality** that it reflects a phenomenon of psychodiversity amongst the population. Everyone's brain is wired differently. Nobody has identical neurological functioning. Some people have a higher level of emotional hypersensitivity than average; some have a more visceral need for intellectual stimuli than others; some are highly reactive to stressful social situations, whilst others are low-reactive, and so on.

Akin to the animal kingdom and plant realm, wherein a *bio*diversity of species exists symbolising the abundance of the living world, there is also a *psycho*diversity[12] in the human species, which shows that we all have a different psychological facet: a unique cognitive profile.

If human nature were only comprised of people who were perfectly balanced psychologically – people with a "normal" level of sensitivity, sociability and intellectual abilities – we would all be identical copies!

Differences are definitely required in order for human society to function in a balanced way overall, where everyone can do their bit. For example, extroverts' gifts in the field of communication and leadership are needed for positions such as managers, heads of communication and sales personnel, whilst introverts' talents are useful for jobs which require more restraint, attentiveness, and analysis, such as a psychologist or an engineer. Society needs introverts who play a role of "social pacifiers" in the jungle of billions of individuals; otherwise the world would be in permanent state of conflict and turbulence. It also needs extroverts who represent an opposite, complementary strength to maintain a dynamic, social balance.

Furthermore, consider the extraordinary abilities of certain high-functioning autistic people (visual thinking, speaking eight languages, reciting vast numbers of decimal points for the number Pi, etc.) which have given rise to inventions or technological innovations in the service of humankind. Similarly, in the history of human evolution, it has required individuals to be born with heightened sensitivity who were more cautious and wary, because in prehistory, if man had lacked any sense of awareness he would have been more vulnerable and exposed to the hazards of his environment. Such general psychodiversity follows a certain evolutionist logic for the survival of the human species.

Psychodiversity or neurodiversity can be defined as a variety of different cognitive ways of functioning which make up human nature. Amongst other psychological labels known to the general public, examples include:

♦ **Hypersensitivity**[13]: This is a character trait, being a form of sensitivity which is far greater than is to be found in most people. Hypersensitive people are often highly-strung; more inclined to have acute emotional reactions; and have increased perceptual acuity which results in their feeling everything more deeply, such as the nuances of their environment, injustice and other people's emotions.

♦ **Intellectual giftedness:** According to the official definition, an intellectually gifted individual has an IQ of 130 or more, and represents 2% of the general population.[14]
At school, an extremely gifted child can be identified when it is evident that he or she is intellectually advanced for his age and demonstrates boundless curiosity, etc.
The image that we have of a gifted individual is often a far cry from reality. On the whole, exceptionally gifted adults are academic and professional failures who find themselves marginalised. They are people of a cerebral nature who like thinking, and they feel a greater need for intellectual stimuli than the average person.

We will not go into the details in each description because that is not the objective of this book which is primarily intended to be a handbook on social communication and not psychology. Indeed, it would be too much of a burdensome task to enumerate every characteristic and every study on this subject. There are already enough books known to the public at large which deal with topics such as introversion, and hypersensitive and intellectually gifted people. Naturally, we will point you to bibliographic references at the end of the book.

This chapter on psychodiversity has but one purpose: to demonstrate that human psychology is complex and, from a neurological point of view, we are all different. To know who we are and how we function is the first phase of integrating into society better.

It is helpful to know whether you tend to be introverted or hypersensitive in order to be aware of the way you function and then learn how to fit in with society more successfully. Yes, some segments of the population are categorised as having greater difficulty in interacting with other people. This is undeniable. There are individuals who have a natural predisposition to chatting, laughing and communicating, whilst others are more inhibited, with this dating from childhood for environmental or genetic reasons. This does not mean that introverts, anxious types or autistic people are not intended to live with others! They can flourish in friendship and love in their own way, within a framework which suits them. To each their own personality; to each their own path.

Deep down, whatever the psychological label, be it nature or nurture, remember this message from the book:

> The main thing is to know oneself and improve one's social communication in order to be in harmony with others.

4) LEARNING HOW TO ACCEPT YOURSELF BETTER: THE TRUE KEY TO A CURE

Many people are convinced that in order to get better and make friends, the solution is to get rid of their introverted character or hypersensitivity for good… Some believe that being serious, reserved, too nice or different from others is the reason why they have little success with people.

It is a mistake to think like this. You only have to look at the thousands of people who are like you with those sorts of character traits and who are in harmony with others all the same.

We need to tell the difference between what we cannot alter (our personality) and what we truly can change (our social communication).

As we have seen previously, introversion is more of a character trait and there is absolutely no use in forcing yourself to become an extroverted person when you are not one! In the end, the issue is not your personality but your social communication.

THE PROBLEMATIC DILEMMA: "PERSONALITY *VERSUS* SOCIETY":

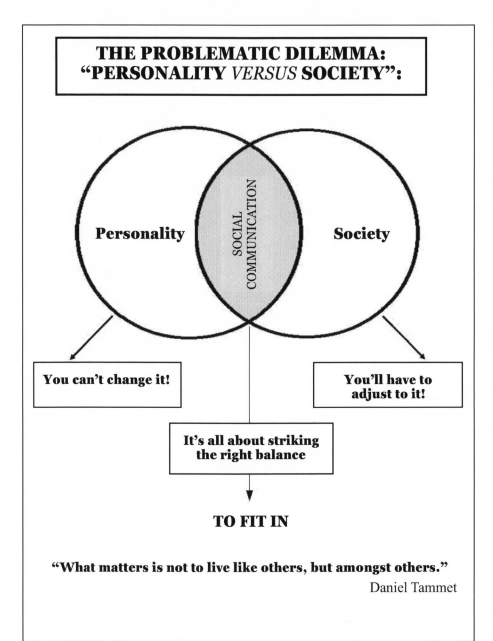

"What matters is not to live like others, but amongst others."

Daniel Tammet

SHOULD THE HEALING OBSESSION BE A GOAL?

We all have our afflictions and personal neuroses which are the root cause of our difficulties in forming relationships with others: poor self-esteem, traumas, upsets, difficult background, and so on. We cannot deny that they exist. Certainly, shyness can get better with practice and age. Anxiety can be controlled with gradual exposure or relaxation. Many of our neuroses can also diminish using techniques on ourselves or the right therapy. However, the will to heal must not become an obsession at the risk of fostering disillusionment as to the achievements in well-being which will perhaps never materialise.

Actually, for most people, the reality is that they will never be fully cured. They will always live with some of their inner demons and maladjusted behaviour. There are handicaps which are not easy to overcome completely, such as social phobia, depression and bipolar disorder. There are stubborn neuroses, traumas which leave lifelong scars and it would be wrong to believe that they can be eradicated in just a few months.

There are those who always see a glass as being half-empty and others who always see it as half-full! Some people are 'high-reactive' to external stimuli, undoubtedly owing to greater activity in their amygdala. Others are 'low-reactive'. Not all of us are equally resilient. We cannot be cured of something which is an integral part of us. There will always be traces or remainders of our past neuroses in our daily behaviour. This is normal and one must come to terms with it.

It is already a formidable victory if a socially phobic person who has always been afraid of others manages to reduce their extreme shyness over the years and thanks to their efforts, they have succeeded in experiencing the joy of love, and finding their place within society. Even though his or her blunders or self-sabotaging thoughts might resurface at any moment, the main thing is not to eliminate them so that they no longer exist, but to tone them down and control them. For this person, true healing does not necessarily mean the disappearance of social phobia symptoms, but instead means the ability to live in harmony with them and not allow this handicap to represent an obstacle to finding a job or friends in life.

It is the same story for a person living with diabetes or heart problems – not everything can be cured. In no way do these health issues prevent him from being happy and making friends in life. It is definitely harder, but it is possible provided that one accepts them and learns to live with them as if they were no longer 'enemies' but 'allies'.

So, rather than struggling to heal at all costs; rather than investing money and tremendous energy in therapies which last an eternity and often lead to nothing, it is good to bear in mind that the key to a cure lies also in your acceptance. This consists of being comfortable with one's individuality, knowing how to live with one's sensitivities and learning how to appreciate them, whilst focusing on positive points and the message they convey for our mission in life on Earth.

Four things are essential for our happiness: a job, a family, friends and an affective life. They are within our reach. They are easier to attain than wearing oneself out in the desperation of searching for a cure. Ultimately, the only thing you can have power over and which allows you to fulfil your desire for happiness is your social communication.

SIX REAL TIPS TO LEARN HOW TO ACCEPT ONESELF BETTER

♦ **Accept that your individuality is part of your nature:**
You are rather introverted or shy. This is the law of psychodiversity. This makes up a part of you and you have to accept it. You are not the only one. There are thousands of people like you around the world who have learned to live in harmony with their individuality.

♦ **You need to realise that people attach more importance to your social communication:**
In any case, most people can see that you are different or that you are somewhat gauche. You too can perceive this in others. It is pointless trying to hide it. In truth, what puts you at a disadvantage most is not your individuality but your lack of social communication.

♦ **Be proud of what you are – turn the lead into gold:**
If you come to terms with your quirks, you will gain a unique facet. Denying that your individuality exists or being ashamed of it will not do you any favours. It will make you feel like a misfit. It is important to accept who you are. Your personality has good points. Make a note of them and keep them in mind. If you have a handicap, find a way of presenting it in a positive, creative light.

♦ **Accept yourself as you would your best friend:**
One is always more demanding of oneself than of others. Try to respect yourself as you would respect your best friend. Even though other people have their faults, you try to understand and accept them. So, make the same effort with yourself.

♦ **Use self-deprecation:**
If you are socially awkward or have particular flaws, make the most of them. Indeed, there are people who come to terms with having their head in the clouds and being fretful or solitary types. They cheerfully make the best of it when they talk about it. This is a radical solution to laugh off their uneasiness and overcome the fear of how other people perceive them.

♦ **Think of the mission as being one of life's messages:**
All your trials and tribulations are part of your story. You have grown up being different. You have to acknowledge it by appreciating it and accepting that, on occasion, you will go through difficult ordeals. There is a meaning to all of this. Remember:
"If you feel like you don't fit into the world you inherited it is because you were born to help create a new one."
Ross Caligiuri, Dreaming in the Shadows

It is quite understandable that for most of us, it is still a tricky thing to accept oneself and view handicaps from an optimistic perspective, especially when we have endured them for such a long time! However, struggling against something which makes up a part of us, or which is integral to our story, ultimately bears no fruit. It necessitates an act of maturity in order to be at peace with oneself.

The aforementioned potential solutions are practical propositions. There is no doubt that those who live contentedly with their individuality have applied at least one of these six 'ingredients'. What is more, there are many real-life examples of celebrities who have come to terms with their flaws: motivational speaker Nick Vujicic born with a congenital disorder characterised by the absence of arms and legs; actress Isabelle Mergault who exploits her dyslalia in her shows; actor Abdé Maziane, a sufferer of ectodermal dysplasia which he makes into a strength and unique feature; comedian and film director Woody Allen who makes no bones about his asocial, anxious, spaced-out personality, and others.

Let us recall these two splendid quotations on the topic of self-acceptance:

"Be yourself; everyone else is already taken." Oscar Wilde.

"Being oneself means being excluded by certain people. Being like others means excluding oneself." Jean Céré.

5) THE SPECIAL CASE OF AUTISTIC PEOPLE

We shall conclude this chapter by examining the case of autistic people suffering from Asperger's Syndrome. This autistic disorder is gaining ever more media coverage. It is a developmental disability characterised by impairment of social interaction and stereotypical behaviour.

Asperger's Syndrome[15]: this is an autism spectrum disorder without intellectual deficiency. According to Dr. Simon Baron Cohen, it is a form of amplification of male cognitive traits (systemising) to the detriment of female cognitive traits (empathy). This would explain their atypical characteristics: repetitive behaviour, a logical, systematic way of thinking, encyclopaedic language, difficulty in putting themselves in another person's position, and so forth.

When we refer to Asperger's Syndrome, some people conjure up the image of the character Rain Man from the famous film, played by actor Dustin Hoffman; that is to say, an asocial, unpredictable human being, possessing exceptional abilities in memory and mental arithmetic. This is somewhat caricatured because most people affected are far from the image some have of the autistic savant. They have no special gifts and do not generally suffer from language deficiency or mental retardation.

Asperger's Syndrome is caused by a neurobiological malfunction, affecting communication skills and social interaction. Autistic people find it hard to grasp social codes: the implicit; non-verbal language; social conventions; humour; emotions, and so on. As a result, making friends and fitting in with a group are not things which come naturally to them and most have learnt how to do this with varying degrees of success, thanks to their upbringing.

For example, if you meet people with Asperger's Syndrome, remember that they are not necessarily shy or reserved. Some might even be chatty and enthusiastic, monopolising the conversation for a considerable time on a specialised topic which fascinates them, such as the economy, IT or architecture. However, during a discussion they may not automatically realise that the person they are talking to is getting bored or showing signs of being peeved. Indeed, they experience difficulties in understanding people's intentions and reading facial expressions.

According to the degree of disability, Asperger's Syndrome can be a stumbling block to fitting in with society. Make no mistake about it – interacting without a social sense, having behavioural peculiarities and poor eye contact are not really going to help a person have normal social interplay with people.

Regardless of the above, there are thousands of adults with Asperger's across the world who have found their place in society and have been able to form social ties. This is another fact not to be overlooked! Quite simply, it is because they have learnt to assimilate social codes and develop their social skills. Despite their quirks, they have the relevant social communication abilities at their disposal to be able to interact with others.

Most of the advice given in this book is, of course, applicable to autistic people and those with Asperger's Syndrome. They can rely on the rules of social 'interactionology' to improve their social life, namely:

- **When you are at a social event** (a party, a conference), the main thing is to display your signs of availability to people to show that you are on the 'human scene'.

- **When you are a victim of the effect of negative social labelling** (i.e., people avoid you and you are regarded as a social outcast), always remember to approach the other person first if he or she does not dare do so. Reassure them by introducing yourself.

- **Often, when you are on a one-to-one basis**, it is hard to have a real interaction because some of the behavioural oddities associated with autism can make the other person feel uneasy and cut the conversation short. However, you can always compensate for your handicaps by making use of other attractive signs of sociability to connect with people.

We are now going to study an example inspired by an autistic person's real-life story.

NEW REAL-LIFE EXAMPLE:
Case study of Jeremy, 28, autistic

Jeremy has Asperger's Syndrome. He is an engineer in a cybersecurity firm. He has a number of handicaps when it comes to his social communication, including constant avoidance of eye contact; strange posture; trouble understanding humour and deciphering other people's emotions. In spite of this, he has integrated into society and is appreciated for his qualities of kindness and courtesy by those around him. He has a few friends whom he met during his studies and over the Internet. He shares hobbies with them, such as chess and board games.

The majority of his friends whom he sees at the weekend are introverted people like himself, who accept that he is different. How can we explain his success in fitting in despite the troublesome hindrances associated with autism? Let us try to fathom out the reason, using our famous Table of the Ten Signs of Sociability.

No.	**SIGNS OF SOCIABILITY**	Attraction Effect	COMMENTS
1	Eye contact	😟✖🧲	As with some autistic people, Jeremy has a great deal of difficulty in maintaining eye contact, which is a real impediment when interacting with others! He does not look them in the eye enough.
2	Smiling		
3	Conversation		Jeremy is able to keep up a conversation. Even though he has a rather slow, monotonous way of speaking, he is very open-minded and able to converse on a number of specialised subjects.
4	Open body language	😟✖🧲	Jeremy absolutely detests physical contact and has a curious posture caused by the rigidity of his body. His facial expressions are frequently unsuitable for the circumstances.
5	Interest in others;	😟✖🧲	As with some autistic people, Jeremy finds it hard to decipher emotions and put himself into another person's position. Nevertheless,

			he does manage to compensate by his great attentiveness.
6	Paying a sincere compliment		
7	Appearing to be conciliatory	☺ ⚡ 🧲	Jeremy stands out because of his good upbringing. He is a courteous man, sometimes too much so. He carefully abides by the rules of politeness. He always remembers to greet people and thank them, and is amenable.
8	Positive mood or sense of humour		
9	Expressing one's gratitude to others	☺ ⚡ 🧲	This is paradoxical: regardless of Jeremy's autism, he shows a lot of compassion. He is always grateful to others, almost mechanically repeating "thank you," and offering little gifts. He knows his friends' birthdays by heart.
10	Taking the initiative; inviting others	☺ ⚡ 🧲	Jeremy dares not make friendly advances to people. He feels more comfortable using texts and e-mails through which he manages to take the initiative, by suggesting dates to his friends for going out.

Conclusion:

Jeremy's case is atypical. As a result of his Asperger's Syndrome, he has odd behaviour patterns and experiences a lot of trouble in maintaining eye contact. This can make people feel uncomfortable. Although Jeremy has a significant handicap, surprisingly enough, he has integrated into society and even formed relationships!

His expert skills in cybersecurity mean he can enjoy employment in a well-known firm. His colleagues appreciate his work and have become used to his atypical personality. Even though a part of his social communication is lacking, he compensates through a whole set of signs of sociability which make him appealing. He is able to converse a little, is exceedingly courteous and, most importantly, shows his gratitude to others. His little tokens of attention, such as presents, sweets, never forgetting friends' birthdays, and his saying "thank you" over and over again can give the impression of being gauche but also make him touchingly benevolent.

Jeremy has learnt all these social codes thanks to his excellent family upbringing. He is always available, accommodating and never turns down any friendly advances. He takes the initiative upon himself by texting and e-mails, suggesting dates to his friends for going out. In conclusion, he manages to harmonise his social relations by using a multitude of signs of sociability. This is the case with thousands of autistic people around the world who succeed in standing out from the crowd by fitting in with others.

CHAPTER VII

SOCIAL COMMUNICATION IN GROUP CONVERSATIONS

1) GROUP CONVERSATIONS: A DIFFERENT DYNAMIC

Group conversations of between three and eight people are altogether different from one-to-one discussions between two people. They take place at lunch breaks at work, in group excursions, and at parties with friends. They possess a different dynamic with a greater need to maintain the conversation and save face in front of other members of the group.

The pressure of how other people perceive you is higher and causes a great deal of problems for many a shy or introverted person! Most feel very ill at ease and cannot bear the shallowness of group conversations because people talk about everything and nothing; interrupt each other; giggle; change subject suddenly, and so forth. People are usually 'giving a performance' as if in a play, and conversations can last so long that we find them wearisome.

For someone who does not talk a lot, he or she can quickly find themselves excluded from the group or even considered to be haughty. Some introverted people constantly force themselves to find things to talk about and relate until they are mentally exhausted and end up going home frustrated and disappointed. Other more asocial types even go so far as to avoid any group situations at all. In our society where interacting with others is a necessity, this is not a solution either.

In this chapter, we shall see that solutions do indeed exist to help you cope in group situations and feel more at ease in conversations, yet not be compelled to speak a lot. Yes! This is possible!

This advice is intended for the most reserved types of people and it can change their lives, because henceforth they will view these group situations with less apprehension and pressure. Likewise, if you have an introverted sibling or child, rather than your just looking on as they avoid joining in at parties with guests at home, this chapter will save them from their discomfort. You will be able to help them fit in with a group using these practical solutions.

2) THE PARTICULAR CASE OF ASOCIAL PEOPLE

There are people who, quite simply, do not like to talk. Group situations are a real ordeal for them. They relish solitude and do not desperately seek the company of others. Such asocial people do exist and there are many of them around the world. In your circle of acquaintances, you are sure to know a colleague at work, a friend or cousin, who is somewhat asocial and has chosen a very stay-at-home lifestyle. Unfortunately, most books of advice on personal development or psychology leave out or neglect asocial types, often providing them with unsuitable socialisation guidance.

First of all, we need to differentiate the two types of introvert: those for whom social contact is a cause of anxiety, who are categorised as shy or socially anxious people; and those for whom social contact is a real bore, who are defined as asocial individuals.

Let us remember that shy people can have fun with others when they feel comfortable and are free from the fear of what other people might think of them. They actively seek out the company of others, going out and socialising. Conversely, asocial people see social interaction as tedious and bothersome. They are only too glad to stay at home or reduce their social life to a strict minimum.

In group situations, asocial individuals prefer to assume their atypical character and do not like to force themselves to play a role or be a chatterbox. They just do not see any point in doing so. It requires them to make an immense effort and they would rather revitalise themselves in silence. They have every right to do this. Nothing obliges them to natter with others, to laugh and gesticulate if they do not feel like it. Naturally, let us respect every one's individual character. That is the way of human nature and it results from psychodiversity. There are people who love chattering and others who do not!

This is a most tiresome problem for an asocial person. There are many social situations where it is impossible to withdraw totally into oneself; otherwise, one would be completely shut off from others. Yet, an asocial person is definitely obliged to live within society, to work to earn a living, and have a few leisure activities to fulfil their personal needs. It requires at least some social communication from them if they want to join a company or sports club, for example!

We shall see that it is entirely possible for an asocial person to "save face" with a group and fit in, provided that he or she follows a few routines in order to preserve group cohesion.

3) THE SOLUTION TO OPT FOR IN A GROUP: AVAILABLE SOCIAL COMMUNICATION

We have all had the experience of meeting someone who is withdrawn and hardly speaks at a social occasion. It did not cause us any particular problem, did it? The reason for this is that deep down, the only risk which an introverted or asocial person runs is being perceived as supercilious by others because of his or her aloof behaviour and obvious silence.

Indeed, bear in mind that what repels people when they meet each other is when a person displays – explicitly and deliberately – all the human signs of unavailability.

These are: *not looking in the eye of the person to whom one is speaking; evident lack of interest in the topic of conversation; externalising one's boredom with sighs; a totally expressionless face; signs of irritation or bitterness, and so on.*

You will agree that the aforegoing rarely occurs amongst people who are the slightest bit civilised! If an individual behaves in this way on purpose, it is reasonable to expect that no one will want to engage them in conversation. Even the most withdrawn human being would never want people to behave with him or her in that manner!

Therefore, one way for an extremely reserved individual to avoid appearing condescending with the other person in a group situation is to use a method called Available Social Communication, as is shown by the following diagram.

WHAT IS AVAILABLE SOCIAL COMMUNICATION? (ASC)

You tend to be an **extremely reserved** type...

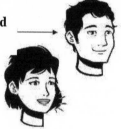

When you're in a group

Having Available Social Communication means adopting some of the following routines:

✓ Smiling when the person speaks to you.

✓ Genuinely listening to others.

✓ Occasionally showing signs of approval (agreement, nodding of the head).

✓ Getting involved in the conversation by asking questions to show one's presence.

✓ Reformulating the other person's last sentence to show that you are listening to them (e.g., "you were saying that...")

 In this way, you don't cut yourself off from other people and you maintain social interaction – that is the main thing!

And that's it! Amazing, isn't it? Every one of these little routines is within everybody's reach. True enough, you will have already met someone at a social occasion who was exceptionally reserved and they behaved exactly in the way mentioned above. In the end, you will have forgiven them for their blunders and wordlessness and the reason for this is that their social communication is proof that they are available to others.

Take careful note of this list of ASC routines – the more they are applied, the more you will affirm your desire to fit in with a group.

There we are. It is no big deal and it something anyone can do, even the most introverted of people. These are small signs of sociability. A winning smile can replace words. Your social communication will then not be closed but remain open. In this way, you will show others that you are still on the scene with them, and you do not scorn them.

If you are an asocial person and you do not like chatting, making use of these little ASC routines means you will both retain the esteem of others and avoid becoming completely cut off from them.

Furthermore, this will help you feel better about your periods of silence and will preclude your having to force yourself to play the role of an extrovert which is not in keeping with your inner personality.

Nothing obliges you to be talkative or laugh if, deep down, you do not feel like it. However, you must do at least the minimum to save face in front of other people so that they are not uneasy in your company.

Using ASC will allow you to feel less pressure from the group and have more peace of mind by coming to terms with your own character. Your friends and colleagues will get used to your persona and gradually learn to accept you as you are. They will adapt to situations where you stay in the background and, with time, they will not even notice anymore.

"By looking at you, they will get used to you". – Quotation from René Char.

4) THE MAIN THING: AVOID CLOSED SOCIAL COMMUNICATION

Here is a table summarising the effects of both available and closed social communication. You can compare them:

Signs	Available Social Communication (ASC)	Closed social communication
Eye contact	Synchronised eye contact with others	Avoidance of eye contact
Smiling	A winning smile	Never smiles
Conversation; interest	Active listening; reformulation; asking questions	Being in one's own world; barely paying attention to conversation
Appearing accommodating	Signs of approval. nodding the head, courtesy	Signs of annoyance, sighs, rejection
Friendly advances	Showing oneself to be open to friendly suggestions	Appearing unavailable, displaying indifference
Consequences on friends and family:	☺⚡🧲 _>> One projects the image of someone who is available and retains the esteem of others!_	☹✖🧲 _>> One projects the image of someone who is haughty, thus cutting him or herself off from others!_

From looking at this table, you will have gathered that what puts people off the most is not your reserve or shyness. It is when a person has social communication which is _deliberately_ closed – that makes people feel most uneasy. Also, nature has not programmed the human being to interact with those who have no social communication!

There are, and there always have been, introverted or asocial people who have fitted in with society and human groups throughout the history of mankind and in every society.

Have you ever met an extremely reserved person at work who spoke very little but, nevertheless, had a charming smile and you felt that they were listening to your every word? Did you hold it against them? No, quite simply because that person did *"communicate" with you, albeit in a different way from your own, but in their unique fashion.*

Moreover, many introverted individuals quickly become uncomfortable and end up adopting erratic behavioural patterns towards the group as soon as they run out of things to say to keep the conversation going:

- Either they start talking a great deal, stammering, and saying any old thing with the sole aim of avoiding gaps in the conversation;

- Or they dig their heels in, get flustered, and experience moments of awkwardness. Additionally, they lose self-confidence in this sort of situation and dwell on their disillusionment even after the occasion has passed.

On the other hand, if a person adopts a simple, light-hearted demeanour and uses ASC routines (for example, smiling, asking a question, or reiterating the other person's last sentence), this immediately revitalises the interaction and helps get out of an embarrassing social situation.

From the moment you begin to "communicate socially" with another person when you meet them, be it discreetly with verbal or non-verbal signals in a coherent, balanced manner, social attraction comes into play and no one will ever be upset by you!

A Rule of Social Interactionology: Sociable people always forgive those extremely introverted people who display Available Social Communication (ASC) in the group – but not those who explicitly and deliberately shut off their social communication.

THINK ABOUT THIS: If there is someone in your circle of friends and family who is asocial and troubled by their isolation, feel free to print out these relevant pages of the book about ASC for him or her. You will be doing them a great service by helping them feel better about their mental blocks and realise that just a few routines are all that is required to succeed in integrating with others!

CHAPTER VIII

CHOOSING A FAVOURITE INTEREST AND GOING OUT TO MEET SUITABLE PEOPLE

1) CHOOSING A FAVOURITE INTEREST TO CREATE MEANING AND SOCIAL TIES

Having a passion for something is vital and fundamental to any type of success; otherwise, life would have no meaning. In order to make friends, you have to start by looking at your pursuits and interests because this is what will give you a good excuse for meeting people and nurturing relationships.

Therefore, a main interest may be used to:

➤ Create meaning: provide an occupation; a leisure activity; a mission in life.

➤ Create social ties: make friends; share activities together.

➤ Preserve well-being: staying focused on a leisure activity prevents you from harking back to some angst or another.

A pursuit remains the best antidote to solitude, as it can create opportunities for meeting people at other places, or occupy you at home and stop you from brooding over negative thoughts.

Pinpointing one's interests is a crucial step for every person. Nonetheless, it can turn out to be a tricky task for some. Either you feel as if you are empty with no pursuits in life, or you have too many different interests and you do not know which ones to pick!

Every human being is bound to have one or more interests, natural skills or is attracted to doing this or that: sport, arts, science, reading, gaming, cinema, music, business, and so on.

Very often, the people who say that they have no passion for anything merely lack self-confidence and are unable to identify what really interests them. They need time and maturity to come to this realisation. However, they are bound to have some activities which they pursue as recreation in their free time.

So, take the time to ponder and pinpoint your interests. Ask yourself what activities you enjoy the most; the ones which have thrilled you ever since your childhood, and which you would like to share with others. List your interests according to your order of importance. This can help you have a clearer picture and get ideas for activities:

MY LIST	MY FAVOURITE PURSUITS AND INTERESTS:
No. 1	
No. 2	
No. 3	
No. 4	
No. 5	

2) GOING OUT; FINDING THINGS TO DO

In order to meet people, obviously, the very first thing to do is create opportunities for going out.

The act of going out does not guarantee that you will meet the right people but if you remain at home all the time, you can be sure that you will not form any real connections! Going out will give you an extra chance of meeting people you like.

The goal is to go to places where you will meet people who are likely to be kindred spirits and have leisure activities in common with you.

Whether or not you set high standards as to the type of people you associate with, somewhere nearby or in your region there are bound to be people with whom you can get along and strike up a great friendship – it has to be so!

Loneliness can be caused by not knowing what to do at the weekend. As a result, a person shuts him or herself off and stays in front of their computer.

The best way to overcome a feeling of loneliness is to have a goal, an activity which stops us from brooding each day.

Here is a list of activities to fill up your weekend which do not automatically come to mind. The aim of this list is not to force these activities on you but rather to suggest ideas!

It is now up to you to pick out an activity from the list which appeals to you that you can suggest to your chums. There must be a pursuit you will enjoy which will give you a reason to go out.

IDEAS FOR ACTIVITIES TO KEEP YOU OCCUPIED!

Recreational activities: fine arts, astronomy, cinema, board games, writing workshops, gardening, music, photography, ecology, scrabble, theatre, arts and crafts, embroidery, sewing, dancing, model making, escape games, boating, lectures, cultural events, going to see a football match, tarot card games, and so on...

Outdoor activities: strolling in a park, visiting a farm, hiking in the woods, group bicycling, collecting chestnuts, fishing in the river, picking a pretty bunch of wild flowers, building a shed, looking for precious stones, etc.

Sports activities: Taï chi chuan, judo, karate, taekwondo, athletics, basketball, badminton, billiards, savate (kickboxing), cycling, horse riding, rock climbing, fencing, dancing, football, gymnastics, handball, krav maga, motorcycling, bodybuilding, swimming, bowls, table tennis, scuba diving, trekking, rugby, tennis, triathlon, volleyball, yoga and relaxation, etc.

3) PRACTICAL WAYS OF GETTING TO MEET PEOPLE EASILY

This section lists all the ways you can meet new people when you are stuck for ideas of how to make friends. This will encourage you to take action. There is no need to take up every suggestion; just go for avenues which inspire you and are in line with your temperament.

As it happens, there are loads of ideas for meeting new people which you will not have thought of. What is more, you do not necessarily have to spend any money! Let's itemise them one by one.

Practical Idea No. 1: Draw on Your Social Network

Your existing friends make it possible for you to meet new friends! Few of you will have thought of this but it is a method which often works. Each one of our friends has their own social network and, amongst their contacts, we have a much better chance of meeting people with whom we will share an affinity. "*My friends' friends are my friends too*," as the adage goes. There must be a good reason why I get along well with a friend, and if they get along very well with another of their own acquaintances, there is more of a chance that I will befriend that person, rather than a stranger I would meet from an outside social circle. We can have pleasant surprises and come across people who have the same interests, values and ideals as we do.

ACTION! Contact a friend in your social circle and suggest to them that they invite you to the next get-together they are organising with their friends. What is more, as they already know and trust you, there is a strong likelihood that they will agree to your request.

Practical Idea No. 2: Meet people in places you are familiar with

I dare say you will not of thought of this one either but there are places where we spend time every week, such as on public transport, in a library, a workplace, bar or café, parks, and so on… And they can also be potential places for meeting people.

The main reason why we meet fewer people in these familiar places than elsewhere is because it is there that we show people the most signs of *unavailability*. We look contemplative; we frown; we are withdrawn into ourselves; our gaze is riveted to our smartphone… You can be sure that it is impossible to create meeting opportunities in these circumstances!

ACTION! Do a test when you go out or take public transport. Replace your usual behaviour with more noticeable signs of availability. Look at people; smile; start a conversation with just a "hello" or a harmless question, and you will have already created a situation where meeting people is easier.

Practical Idea No. 3: Join an association or club which ties in directly with one of your interests

The best way to meet the right sort of people is to take our interests and hobbies as a starting point. You are bound to have an interest, a pastime or a personal cause which you hold dear. It might be the guitar, badminton, ecology, meditation, board games or writing. Instead of pursuing these interests on your own, you have the option of sharing them with people who have the same areas of interest as yourself. Conversation will be made all the easier and far more spontaneous. In this way too, friendships can be formed by regularly taking part in activities together.

ACTION! Leaf through directories of associations and clubs. Go on Google and type in keywords, such as [*your area of interest*] + *association or club* + [*your town*]. Try a number of searches and then contact the clubs to participate in their events.

Practical Idea No. 4: Take part in your town's cultural events

The many facilities in your town or region (town hall, multimedia library, schools, sports centre, music school, etc.) put on cultural events from time to time where you might meet people. These can be free workshops, exhibitions, open days, concerts, buffets and lectures.

ACTION! When you go out, visit all these various places. Pause and read noticeboards and posters carefully to gather useful information. Take a notepad and jot down the time and date of cultural events so that you do not miss them.

Practical Idea No. 5: Use Internet and Social Networks

There is a staggering number of websites which make it easy for people to meet each other. The Internet is brimming with top tips and tricks of every type to help you get out and about in your town and choose events to suit your tastes.

ACTION! Sign up to these websites below and try them out. We have selected a list of the most popular, well-liked websites for going out and meeting people.

Website:	URL:	Info: [Some of these websites are international and others focus on one country.]
Meetup	www.meetup.com	Meet people who share a particular interest.
Facebook	www.facebook.com/groups	Look at the *Events* section in a Group.
Let's Go Out	www.letsgoout.co.uk	Exciting things to do near you.
Next Door	www.nextdoor.com	Next Door connects neighbours and communities with each other.
Friend Match	www.friendmatch.com	An international social networking service helping people to meet friends.
Polyglotclub	www.polyglotclub.com	Make friends whilst learning a new language.
Bumble	www.bumble.com	An app for finding friends, love and more.
Skout	www.skout.com	International platform to connect people.
Together Friends	www.togetherfriends.com	A friendship site for women to connect and chat.
Worldpackers	www.worldpackers.com	A platform to connect travellers seeking to exchange skills for accommodation.
Couchsurfing	www.couchsurfing.com	Travel, stay with people or share your home. See the *Activities/Events* section.
CitySocializer	www.citysocializer.com	A virtual events platform, network and community.
Meetup for Seniors	www.meetup.com/topics/over-60-social-club	The Over-60s Social Club worldwide.
Autistic Dating	https://autisticdating.net	Dating for people on the autistic spectrum.

Lastly, you can also meet people who are like you or who share the same interests as you by visiting the many discussion forums which exist on the Web. Most of these provide "Meet-up" sections. Go to Google and type the following keywords in: *[your topic or interest] + Forum.*

Or you can go and look at Facebook Groups which are more lively and sometimes organise outings for members interested in the same subject.

For example, on Facebook type the following keywords into the search field under Groups: *Maidstone, ecology, skateboarding, DIY, naturopathy, alternative medicine, etc.*

Er, what should I do if I want to go out but I don't like people?

There are two potential reasons why you do not like people.

1. You have gone through some relationship-related trauma and a lot of rejection and disappointment. As a result, you have decided to put up your guard. This means that there is self-analysis and therapy to be carried out first.

2. Perhaps you have not yet met the right kind of people. It can be easier to open up to people we meet if they are like us or share the same interests.

Are you sure that there is nobody you like on this planet?! That is hardly likely. We cannot like everybody but there have to be some people we do like and who restore our faith in humanity. Therefore, your mission is to find and meet these good people.

4) MAKING FRIENDS BY MEETING THE RIGHT PEOPLE

The right people are those you are likely to get along with 'like a house on fire' and will want to see again to chat with or share activities.

Maybe you do not feel like going out day after day to meet everybody in sight, but just need to meet *appropriate* people.

As awkward as you might be, whether or not you are a very special or atypical character there are suitable people out there who will form a friendship with you. There are billions of individuals on Earth and there are bound to be people who will understand you and share the same values or even your craziest dreams!

Perhaps you have even come across such people already in your life? Although they are few and far between, it means that they do indeed exist somewhere on Earth, be it in your town or region.

So, the question really is: *How* does one go about finding these suitable people?

Now, ask yourself these questions: *Where do the people I'm looking for go? What type of place do they frequent? What are their interests and the things they usually do?*

As we shall see in the next chapter dedicated to Friendship, in order to make true friends and create a solid bond, the deciding factors remain the points you have in common and having a good reason for seeing each other regularly.

If you focus on that, you will maximise your chances of meeting the right people.

Interests and pursuits remain the main lever you can count on, by which you can begin to meet suitable people.

Examples:
- If you live in Brighton and love extreme sports, do a search of your region for your particular interest: clubs, local adverts, use a website such as LetsGoOut.co.uk, Facebook Groups for extreme sports, etc.

- If you live in Tunbridge Wells and are a sensitive, cerebral person, preferring intellectual or cultural excursions, opt for: local lectures and seminars, exhibitions, websites for creative interchange, entrepreneurship groups on Meetup, Facebook Groups or forums for intellectually gifted individuals, and others.

In any case, whoever you are, there will always be one or more solutions available as soon as you decide to become active and meet people.

The more accurately you target specific groups based on your interests, the better your chances are of meeting the right people.

If you put all these ideas and potential solutions earnestly into practice, then you should not find yourself spending weekends feeling isolated anymore!

CHAPTER IX

FRIENDSHIP:
HOW TO MAINTAIN A RELATIONSHIP

1) WHY IS IT IMPORTANT TO HAVE FRIENDS?

Everyone will have their own definition of friendship or of the word friend. It all depends on our wants and needs in regard to human relationships. However, one thing we can all agree on is that it is important to have friends, whether it is to share leisure activities together or to count on during life's little mishaps.

We all have said about a friend on one occasion or another, *"Thankfully, he was there for me." "She's my best friend." We have a good laugh together." "We have no secrets from each other..."* and so on.

Some people obsessively seek love to satisfy an emotional deficit or want to have a pet to make up for their loneliness, when having a real friend in whom they could confide would be a tremendous help to them.

Friendship is one of those conditions for an individual's happiness on a par with love or family. Here are various reasons demonstrating why it is essential to have friends:

> ➤ Human beings need to have leisure activities to occupy themselves or have fun. And these are things we usually do with our friends!

> ➤ Friends contribute greatly to our well-being. They are also the people who make us laugh, or listen to what we have on our mind, and who give us encouragement with our projects. When love fades in a relationship, people separate for good; whereas with a friendship, people can retain a lasting bond.

> ➤ At difficult times when you find yourself alone and isolated, a friend's support can be crucial.

Today, with the boom of the Internet and social networks, it has become very easy to meet people and make connections with a few clicks of a mouse. However, it is much harder to nurture a friendly relationship because most of our encounters in the city are brief or transitory.

In days gone by, we lived in more of a community based on traditional values. We had more occasion to keep seeing people, to visit folks in the same place and share tasks together. This made it possible to forge strong, long-lasting bonds. Modern societies tend to be characterised by weakened community ties in favour of personal interests and consumerism. Therefore, in order to maintain a friendship, it is vital to restore meaning to the relationship which binds two people.

2) CONSISTENCY:
AN ESSENTIAL CRITERION IN DEFINING FRIENDSHIP

Throughout our lives, we may very well have met many new people and come across individuals we click with immediately… Yet, it is much more difficult when it comes to maintaining that friendly relationship!

For most people, making friends comes naturally and effortlessly. For introverted or shy types, it is a lot more complex to begin with because they do not know how to go about things. They meet some great people when they go out socially or to parties. They have a series of fascinating conversations but it stops there in spite of all good intentions…

We are now going to see what the fundamentals are which enable a social contact to blossom into a friendship! Yes, we are not necessarily aware of it; we believe that everything happens by itself and that it is just a question of feeling, but, in fact, there are circumstances which do foster the creation of a true relationship.

So, the definition of a friend can be highly subjective and vary from one person to another. For some, friendship is a strong emotion of reciprocal fondness. It cannot be controlled and may grow or decline depending on each person's stage of life and preoccupations. Contact with a friend can be lost without calling into question the bond of friendship. For others, a friend is just a pal with whom they share pastimes and partying and they do not automatically feel the need to develop deep ties. Lastly, there is the 'legacy friend' who reminds us of our roots or who has shared with us an important time in our life; the childhood friend or the "brother or sister in misfortune" who helped us out.

Every person will have his or her own interpretation and concept of friendship. **Our expectations and needs are not the same** and we have to respect that fact.

 However, this book is intended for a sensitive readership who are facing challenges in forming true friendships and endeavouring to understand how to maintain a bond. As such, we willingly come out in favour of a clear, more objective definition so that we can provide you with the best of solutions!

> For the sake of clarity, what we mean when we say 'friend' is someone with whom we wish to maintain ties and interact with on a regular basis at the very least.

Indeed, it makes no sense to call a person "a friend" if we never see them physically and never talk to them either on the phone or via the Internet. Perhaps they were a friend in your childhood or at a previous time in your life, but, as of today, they are real friends no longer; they just remain a legacy friend. Therefore, an authentic friend is first and foremost someone with whom you talk regularly outside of the work or school context. Here we have a simple, reasonable criterion by which we can recognise a true friend as distinct from a casual chum.

The best friends are those who are available. They cannot resist calling each other or writing from time to time because they have things to tell one another. People who are not friends are content just to send messages out of courtesy but they have no reason to correspond regularly with each other!

You can get along with someone very well, have lots in common, and have a good laugh together. However, if you never interact or only do so occasionally every five years, for instance, then there is no reason to consider this relationship as a friendship in the true sense of the word because **it is not really being kept up**. True friends are above all those with whom we have a continuous relationship.

Based on this pragmatic, requisite definition, which relates to the ideal friendship everyone is looking for deep down, it becomes a lot easier for every one of us to understand how to make friends and, most importantly, maintain a bond.

So, there must be a 'reason' for two people keeping in touch regularly; an emotional purpose which encourages them to want to see each other or to engage in lively discussion. If there is no 'reason,' be it a pastime or a shared goal with someone, then it seems unlikely that this person will become your best friend – it is as simple as that!

There are two universal criteria which help a friendship to blossom:

- ✓ Things in common

- ✓ Physical or geographical proximity

It would seem impossible from the start for two people to become friends if they have nothing in common, such as an interest, a leisure pursuit, an objective or shared values.

Physical or geographical proximity helps reinforce a bond because it means people can see each other repeatedly and share activities, even though this is no longer a 'must' in our modern epoch with the growth of the Internet and mobile telephones. 'Remote' friendships can also exist, provided that the criterion of consistency is adhered to and that people do interact with each other often, at the very least.

Conclusion: If you want to make true friends, make a point of looking for people in your geographical region who have the same interests or the same goals as you.

Following this, find a good reason for you to see one another frequently. The more you interact with someone, the more you strengthen the bond with them.

3) THREE THINGS WHICH ENCOURAGE
A CONSISTENT RELATIONSHIP

You will have now come to understand that you cannot maintain a relationship if there is not at least regular contact with a person.

If both individuals remain passive and there is no reason for seeing each other again, the whole thing will be pointless even if there is wonderful chemistry between you. Your relationship will never get further than the mere 'acquaintance' stage.

Therefore, the question we should really be asking ourselves is, *"What would make it possible for me to develop a consistent relationship with this person?"*

There are at least three answers to this question and we will list some ideas:

> **A conversational topic about something you are keen on** which prompts each person to call or write to one another regularly.

> **A leisure activity to pursue together:** games, sport, music, cooking, IT, going out to the cinema, artistic activities, etc.

> **A shared project:** creation of an association or a business together, shooting a short film, preparing for a trip, having the goal of losing weight together, and so on.

A pursuit is an excellent reason for seeing each other at the weekend and having fun together. A shared project can lend more depth to a relationship and help it thrive into the future. In any case, it maintains a bond.

This advice is all the more applicable if you have a friend who tends to be introverted or shy. Often, reserved people are not very talkative in daily life, but when they speak about their interests, they become a lot more effusive. They prefer genuine, deep relationships.

Look at all the wonderful examples of friendship around you – people who are friends, not simply because they get along well but because they see one another often and they create projects together. They have things to recount and share together. Their bond is maintained over time.

This is demonstrated by some examples of famous friendships: Leonardo DiCaprio and Tobey Maguire, Matt Damon and Ben Affleck, Mel Gibson and Robert Downey Jr., Lionel Messi and Luis Suarez, Jennifer Aniston and Courteney Cox...

4) LITTLE ROUTINES TO MAINTAIN A FRIENDSHIP

Despite everything, there is another reality which one cannot ignore. Specific situations in life can considerably complicate and diminish your social life: *a time-consuming job of work, moving house, married life, the children, retirement, illness, depression, and so on.*

Each person's preoccupations vary depending on their stage of life and contribute to people gradually growing apart even though they might have built up a solid friendship.

In view of this, the best remedy for preserving the flame of friendship remains following a leisure pursuit or doing a project together.

You might notice a friend becoming more distant because they have got married and had children. If you remain totally passive, then you can be sure that you will lose this friend because the events of life and your different respective concerns will sooner or later result in splitting you up.

However, if you decide to be proactive and take the initiative to find ideas for pastimes or simply ask how they are getting on, then you will help to continue this great friendship.

That is why there are many people in their thirties and forties who are still very good friends, in spite of their own family life and job, because they have kept up the relationship with regular contact.

The various concerns of everyday life (family, money, new areas of interest) are enough to drive people apart very quickly, but taking part in shared activities helps sustain friendship.

Moreover, it is best to aim to strengthen ties with a few people who mean something to you, rather than making a lot of friends and going out all the time all over the place. This is because behaving in such a way will not help you keep the best friendships going.

We will now see what simple actions you can take to sustain a friendship. In fact, there are some rather obvious things to do but we do not necessarily think of them or we forget about them! It is good to bear these in mind, using the following summary diagram.

THE FOUR BASIC ROUTINES TO SUSTAIN A FRIENDLY RELATIONSHIP

REMEMBER!
If you can't manage to keep up
a friendship, ask yourself:

HAVE I THOUGHT OF...

✓ Keeping in contact using a particular medium such as mobile phone, e-mail, Skype?

✓ Asking how the person is doing?

✓ Suggesting you meet up

✓ Sharing a pastime or a shared project?

YOUR INTERESTS remain **the main factor** in helping you maintain a relationship and are a good reason for seeing each other!

If you are unable to keep up a relationship with a friend, ask yourself whether you have followed these four basic actions! Many people say they do not know how to maintain a friendship but they do not even apply the fundamentals, despite the mutual affinity they have and things shared in common.

There are countless opportunities for getting back in touch with others and even giving them a nice surprise, for example: *sharing an article which may interest your friend; wishing them a happy birthday or happy new year; asking whether they have resolved their worries; inviting them to the cinema or to do a spot of sport with you, etc.*

 Social networks can help you keep in touch, but...

New technology has made it extremely easy to keep in contact with the people whom you meet: *Facebook, Skype, Messenger, WhatsApp, Instagram, WeChat,* etc. Most of these apps help you get news about your friends from their timeline and give you good reasons for engaging in conversation with them. This method is not to be overlooked, provided that you do not keep chat solely in the virtual domain!

<u>Advantages of Social Networks</u>:
- We can keep track of people whereas without these tools we would have permanently lost touch with them.
- We can get news about our friends from their timeline, photos and messages.
- We can forge new relationships and strengthen existing ones via chats.
- We can get back in touch with lost friends.

<u>Drawbacks of Social Networks</u>:
- It is addictive and an enormous amount of time can be spent on it.
- We can build up numerous contacts and forget to focus on those which are important.
- There is a risk of concentrating on virtual conversations at the expense of meeting people in person.

The main thing is to find a balance and use social networks to keep in touch, and remember to take the initiative to see people and share activities in person.

5) HOW TO STRENGTHEN A RELATIONSHIP: FRIENDSHIP IN THE TRUE SENSE OF THE WORD?

Friendship, like love, is, nevertheless, not a matter of trivial banter or small talk, such as chatting about what's happening or the weather. Banal discussions usually take place when you are with your pals or colleagues at work!

There is something more profound in friendship. Conversations are of a more personal and genuine nature than otherwise. What distinguishes a friendship from mere camaraderie is not only the consistency of interaction but also the human depth of the bond.

When people are asked what they consider to be a true friend, amazingly, most give the following answer spontaneously:
"A true friend is there in bad times as well as good." "A true friend is someone you can count on and call even at difficult times."

These answers demonstrate people's expectations and show that 'being there' and providing support remain the strongest indicators of a real friendship in the collective psyche.

Here is a new diagram to put you in the picture about friendship…

A FEW LITTLE ROUTINES TO STRENGTHEN A FRIENDSHIP

TO FORM A STRONG BOND...

There are things you can do
to get closer to another person:

- ✓ Talking about yourself in a genuine way
- ✓ Taking a sincere interest in the other person
- ✓ Being available if need be
- ✓ Expressing your appreciation of the other person
- ✓ Being able to please people and be of service
- ✓ Having the courage to ask

<u>IMPORTANT</u>: Use the Practical Info Sheets at the end of the book to understand and put each routine into practice.

Indeed, these routines have not been randomly selected and each one is of a particular significance.

If you are only content to talk about your job or entertainment, then the relationship will remain dull. It is essential to open up, share one's feelings and speak about more personal subjects, such as our moods, secrets, dreams and our real worries...

It is equally necessary to take a genuine interest in the person to whom you are talking: discovering their interests, goals in life, their background and needs...

Only in this way do we create **a real connection** with the other person because we learn to know each other mutually and no longer just present a smiling façade for one another.

The difference between a friendship and a casual camaraderie lies in our ability to show our real selves!

SOMETHING TO MEDITATE ON
SO YOU HAVE NO REGRETS...

In the famous bestseller, *The Top Five Regrets of the Dying*,[16] a nurse in palliative care recorded in a notebook the regrets most often expressed by her patients in the last moments of their lives. Amongst the five most common regrets, two were:
"I wish I had stayed in touch with my friends."
"I wish I'd had the courage to express my feelings."

To go further than a shallow relationship, you must be able to express your appreciation for others; that is to say, show people how much they mean to you. If you behave like a colleague, then you will be 'colleagues'. If you behave like a friend, then you will be 'friends'.

For instance, let your friend know that his or her being there means a lot to you. Pay them a few compliments. Thank them when they help you. You will be pleasantly surprised at their reaction. This makes it possible for the other person to know how much they mean to you, because if you do not say it, they will not know and will not be aware of it. This does matter, and it helps in some sort of way to "formalise" the friendship in the other person's mind.

Generally speaking, when people are colleagues or simply buddies, they are not aware of the real moods and troubles we experience in our private lives. They do not know about any of our potential worries, doubts and sadness. However, between friends, we feel free to talk about these things and from time to time to please our friends by doing them favours or giving them tokens of affection. We are there for them both in times of joy and sorrow.

This is all part of friendship – receiving help whilst also being unafraid to ask for it.

At the end of the book, we have added around ten info sheets which will give you ideas for talking about yourself; learning to take an interest in others; knowing how to please people, etc. These info sheets are comprehensive and detailed with the aim of helping you apply all the aforementioned advice.

Don't make assumptions!
DON'T BE AFRAID TO ASK

"My friends go quiet and forget me when I need them."

It can often happen that friends are busy or that they do not show their feelings to you enough. This does not necessarily mean that they have lost interest in you, but they might be powerless to help out or do not know how to go about it. You have to help them to help you.

Likewise, most of the time we expect the person to guess our needs if they are really close to us, and for them to offer their help automatically. It is a mistake to think this way. Often, we dare not ask out of fear of bothering someone or being turned down. However, we might be surprised at the generous reaction of the other person if only we had the courage to ask!

Never make any assumptions (he doesn't like me; he must be too busy, and so on), because you risk wasting your time and upsetting yourself. Always remember to *ask* people for what you want in order to prevent misunderstandings. Many issues which occur in friendship can be resolved and arguments avoided, by **asking in a direct way**.

If you need to see a friend, *don't be afraid to ask when he or she is available.*
If you need help, *go ahead and ask for it.*
If you want more appreciation, *let them know.*

If your friend still doesn't get the picture, *have a good five to ten-minute talk with them* to explain everything and share your feelings. This won't fail to move them and will make them react.

The act of asking does not guarantee that your friend will accede to your requests, but the chances of their taking action will increase and, at least, they will know what's going on. It is vital to be clear with your friends and not be afraid of expressing your expectations — because they cannot guess what they are!

In the end, whatever you ask for, your friend is free to take action or not. **You will have done your part** in your social communication and you will have nothing to regret.

6) OVERALL CONCLUSION: FROM FIRST CONTACT TO FRIENDSHIP...

Here is a final chart to help you come to a realisation and not miss out on meeting people. We may well read loads of advice and think that we have understood, but sometimes we still forget the basics, or we do not think of these things later on!

Therefore, the following table serves as a reminder to you not to remain passive and make you fully aware of the potential reasons for your relational failures.

Do the test by ticking the boxes in the summary table.

SOCIAL INTERACTION TEST:
WHY CAN'T I MAKE FRIENDS?

My checklist to help me identify my mistakes

1st Stage: **HAVING A SIMPLE FRIENDLY INTERACTION**	TICK	Eliminatory mark!
First of all, have you gone out to meet people?		/ / / / /
Did you approach the person?		/ / / / /
Were you smiling?		
Did you take an interest in that person?		
Did you chat about your interests?		
If there was a lull in conversation, did you remember to…		
…reiterate what they had just said so that they carried on talking to you?		
…start off the conversation again with an open question?		
…revive the conversation by talking about yourself (I + a sentence) or by recounting an anecdote?		
2nd Stage: **FORMING A REAL BOND WITH THE PERSON**		
Have you tried to find out what they're really like?		
Have you talked enough about yourself so that they can get to know you?		
Have you highlighted something you have in common (interests, goals, values, etc.)?		
Have you expressed a positive emotion towards them (a compliment, token of attention, appreciation, etc.)?		
Do you often ask how they're doing (on the phone,		/ / / / /

by e-mail, Messenger, etc.)?		
Are you taking any practical initiatives (leisure activities, project, invitation to meet up)?		/////
This chart will help you become aware of what you're doing (or are not doing!) to form and maintain a relationship.		

CHAPTER X

FRIENDSHIP AND SOCIAL INTERACTION IN OTHER CULTURES

Depending on the country and culture, forming a friendship might not be an easy matter. As stated at the beginning of the book, the idea is not to elaborate too much on the differences in cultural codes according to country as this would be an extremely complex task. This book is aimed primarily at an audience interested in human relations in the Western world, particularly Europe and North America.

Even so, we shall add a special supplement and examine friendships in other cultures, so that we can have a broader view and make parallels with the book's fundamental tenets. For example, in Japan it is not quite as easy to make friends as it is in France or the United States. Cultural codes are very different. Over there, people are more reserved and self-restrained when it comes to expressing things of a personal nature.

There is a greater need to 'save face' in Asia than in Europe. This involves having a sociable personality and making a good impression on people when in conversation. Each person respects the other's culture and avoids causing the other person to lose face or embarrassing them. Sometimes, communication is made in a courteous, indirect manner in order to avoid conflict. People tend to talk less about themselves or their troubles for fear of making the other person feel uncomfortable.

Accordingly, most of the socialisation tips written in this book are not applicable abroad. In Asia, tactile contact between people is disapproved of and even seen as intrusive, whereas it is seen as a sign of warmth in some other places, such as in Europe or Africa. In Japan, solitude has even become a real societal problem, an extreme symbol of which is the well-known phenomenon of Hikikomori ("pulling inward, being confined"), which describes those Japanese individuals who live cut-off from the world. They may live isolated at home for months on end or even years. This can be accounted for by a number of sociocultural factors, including addiction to the Internet, and inordinate social pressure to succeed in one's professional life which weighs down on them. Those who fail feel a terrible sense of shame so intensely that they withdraw from society. As social interaction in Japan is influenced by the concept of "saving face," it becomes embarrassing for those Japanese who are unemployed or have no job security.

Conversely, Americans and Brazilians tend to be on familiar terms as soon as they meet each other and smile easily even at strangers. They are quick to ask personal questions, share details about their lives, make jokes, and are tactile. Yet, this does not mean that they want to be friends with you. For them, it is a way of being sociable. A Russian or an Arab traveller can easily be disconcerted by such familiarity right from the start, by the Brazilian waiter's beaming smile, for instance!

Elsewhere, in some American Indian tribes, for example, people do not speak much, only briefly, and never to engage in small talk. When they eat together, they avoid talking, preferring to focus on the present moment, nature and the food. For Native Americans, silence is normal and they cannot understand Westerners who feel the constant need to fill in the gaps.

Lastly, although it might already be a tricky matter for us to make friends in our own country, it can be even more so when we go to stay abroad. For instance, a French student in Asia looking to establish closer ties with other students might think a Chinese or Korean person is very nice and polite during straightforward interactions. However, due to cultural barriers, they will appear suspicious and aloof when the student tries to make friends with them.

This array of examples demonstrates that the rules of socialisation vary greatly from one country to another. Cheerful, tactile behaviour, which is deemed to be sociable here might be frowned on elsewhere. No single rule exists whereby any individual on Earth can easily connect with another. That having been said, human beings are equipped with innate human signals for communication (eye contact, smiling, and gestures). It is just that every culture uses them in a different way depending on context and background.

Social instinct is fundamental to every human being. Human signals exist to allow an individual to interact within society. Speech and gestures are made for communicating with others. As we have seen in previous chapters, human signals can play a dual role. They serve to show whether we are available or not in a particular territory (signs of availability), or to form a social bond (signs of sociability).

Each culture will always have its own natural and divergent codes. Be that as it may, within every culture, specific codes do exist which foster social harmony and better integration with others. More than anything, this is what we must grasp and assimilate so that every person can find their own place within their community.

CHAPTER XI

ACTIVATE RESILIENCE THROUGH SOCIAL INTERACTION; GIVE MEANING TO ONE'S LIFE THROUGH OTHER PEOPLE

Resilience refers to the ability to overcome challenging ordeals, unease and traumatic situations.[17]

Everyone, at some time in their life is going to have to contend with a difficult event. There are people who manage to be happy and surmount their problems (e.g., dyslexia, anxiety, failure and trauma). They have learnt to control them and be resilient over the years.

Then, there are others who continue to suffer, remaining locked into a lifetime of neuroses and discontent without ever succeeding in finding solutions to get along better.

Why do some people manage to "get cured" whilst others do not although they have the same symptoms? We often mistakenly think that the more the symptoms of an illness worsen (diabetes, depression, social phobia), the harder a person will find it to pull through and be happy. This is not necessarily so. Resilience factors are the most important thing. Some people conquer their problems thanks to individual qualities or opportunities provided by their environment.

Resilience factors are the things which help a person develop a means of defence and 'bounce back' despite their daily turmoil. These can be inward in nature (such as perseverance, intrapersonal intelligence and imagination) or external (privileged social background, family support, therapist, and so on).

When a person suffers terribly from loneliness and is brought down every day by negative or suicidal thoughts, it is truly hard to find the strength to pull through. The person might well read loads of books on personal development, explore this or that therapy, do a bit of theatre or yoga from time to time, and indeed feel a few scant moments of joy, but the torment of inner unhappiness quickly catches up with them again.

It is far from easy to live with the burden of a disability, secrets, and traumas on a daily basis. The degree of suffering can be such that it negates every single one of our efforts and plunges us into the vicious circle of our bad habits. We find ourselves to be dull and useless and we constantly compare ourselves with people who have more success than we do. We are haunted by failure or traumatising memories of the past. We are ashamed of ourselves when we are with others. What we must understand is that such circumstances make resilience exceedingly hard to attain. So, highly effective solutions to remedy this have to be found.

To overcome the feeling of angst, it is crucial firstly, to create situations which will assist one's ability to bounce back; and secondly, develop solutions so that one is not upset by the vagaries of everyday life. Effective strategies do exist and these are definitely the best way to reorganise one's life and get back onto the road to happiness.

If there were one lesson you should remember from this book more than all the other advice, it would be this: there are <u>three universal levers which can activate resilience</u>.

♦ **Create meaning:** find your magic domain; an interest or goal which you care about on a daily basis.
♦ **Conquer loneliness:** make friends based on your shared interests and meet the right sort of people.
♦ **Learn to accept yourself:** come to terms with your vulnerabilities and do not feel ashamed in front of others.

These three vital levers have already been broadly expanded upon in the book and show the importance of SOCIAL INTERACTION in the healing process. They summarise this handbook's philosophy which is to strive for social harmony.

In plain language, if you put them into practice you will increase your chances of improving your situation and getting back on your feet. You cannot feel better and heal if you stay alone in your little corner without any goal in life — quite simply, it is impossible. When we are depressed and our brain mulls over the same black thoughts all day long, we are not in a mood to do anything whatsoever — we procrastinate and stay in our bubble.

Therefore, highly positive situations need to be created so that you do not feel overwhelmed by every tinge of the blues which comes along. Only these three crucial levers are truly effective and powerful enough to help you lead a better life and make progress on the path of resilience.

THREE CRUCIAL LEVERS
TO FOSTER RESILIENCE

So that you don't get overwhelmed by angst,
don't forget these rules:

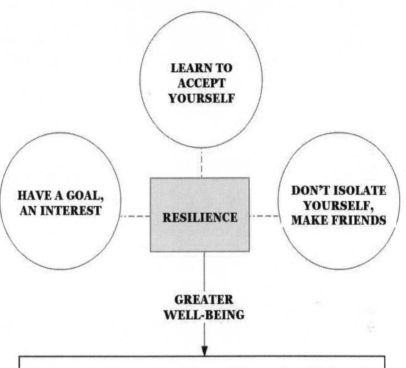

LEARN TO ACCEPT YOURSELF

HAVE A GOAL, AN INTEREST

RESILIENCE

DON'T ISOLATE YOURSELF, MAKE FRIENDS

GREATER WELL-BEING

These are the three major pillars which you should rely on to provide balance in your life.

If you're not following the rules in two of these circles, it means you have a problem situation and need to take action!

Having a set goal or an interest is essential because it gives meaning to your life. It gives you a reason for hope and waking up in the morning. Every day, our thoughts are focused on THIS GOAL, this occupation, which does us good instead of drifting off into negative thoughts. It is the best way to conquer depression. When we do not have a clear goal in life and waste our days away, it is quite normal for us to feel bad psychologically and not have the wherewithal to put up with our unhappiness. Having a goal or an activity to occupy us on a regular basis is a deciding factor in learning to live with objectivity. It is all about finding "our magic domain" and pinpointing that pursuit which will do us good and can be done smoothly and effortlessly. Every individual has a magic domain where they feel comfortable, happy, and in which their state of motivation helps them achieve their full potential. For some, the magic domain could be a creative activity, such as music; whereas for others it could be a sport.

It is even better if we can share activities with people we like. Isolation prevents resilience and keeps us trapped in our bubble with our recurring, negative thoughts. It is vital to have at least a few friends in whom you can confide and with whom you can share the way you feel – you will feel a whole lot better. Connecting with people, going out, meeting people who have the same interests as you is more thrilling and will give you a greater lust for life! It is often said that love can help heal wounds and cure neurosis – the same goes for friendship. When we are cut off from others, our lives slow down and the slightest activity requires psychological effort. When we do have at least a few pals and when we get support from a friend, suddenly everything becomes easier and smoother. We are better able to go about our daily lives, embark on projects and have fun.

Alone, I can't carry on; with others I'm resilient.

Lastly, coming to terms with oneself better is the key to resilience. This core concept has been extensively covered in the chapter on psychodiversity. Accepting one's vulnerabilities and not disowning them is an essential pre-condition for living a happy life. The feeling of shame prevents resilience. Harbouring sad secrets and concealing your faults at all costs keep you in state of angst and constant fear of the way people perceive you. Accordingly, you must learn to accept your flaws and even grow fond of them.

Incidentally, the art of *kintsugi* is a wonderful metaphor for resilience. It is the traditional Japanese art of repairing a broken item by highlighting the breakage lines with gold instead of disguising them. The object's past, its history and any accidents are accepted and displayed. The ceramic item's cracks are shown off proudly with golden joins.

You might be avoiding people because you are worried they will discover your shortcomings, but sooner or later they will find out anyway. However, if you accept your faults and embrace them proudly as an integral part of your 'history', then there is a good chance that they will be viewed more leniently by others. Being in harmony with one's vulnerabilities creates circumstances more favourable for one's own resilience.

CHAPTER XII

HOW TO HELP AN EXCLUDED PERSON INTEGRATE BETTER,

HOW TO HELP OTHERS WELCOME ME INTO THE FOLD

1) EXPERIENCING EXCLUSION: A FEELING OF INJUSTICE

Finding one's place amongst others is every individual's main concern. The following is a typical scene we have all experienced. We see our chums cheerfully chatting and laughing away amongst themselves, while we feel shut out and invisible to them. Sometimes, it can be hard to fit in with a group at work or on friendly outings. We can find ourselves ignored or see another member of the group being excluded.

There can be a variety of reasons for this, for example, unease, shyness, lack of communication, people's apathy, and so on. Nonetheless, the result remains the same. It causes a profound feeling of sadness and anguish in the person concerned. This is the worst thing which can happen at work or when going out: exclusion. It cannot necessarily be perceived but the isolated person suffers inwardly and puts on a brave face.

To give an example, in a business, an excluded colleague will take out his or her frustrations in one way or another, including carelessness at work, absenteeism, being late, not participating in company life, having the impulse to spread rumours, and mixing with other marginalised employees.

Whether it is in the professional, social or family circle, exclusion generates feelings of frustration in the person (aggression, withdrawal into oneself), with unpleasant effects on the general ambience. It is preferable to reduce issues of exclusion as much as possible.

Yet, this is precisely the problem. In a group situation, the people present often look on powerless to do anything about one of their own being shut out, witnessing his or her unease and not knowing what to do or say to help them fit in better.

Yet, solutions do exist which help everybody avoid these distressing predicaments. It only takes a few seconds to utter a comforting sentence or simply proffer a kind human gesture! These are little routines everyone can do to foster social harmony and which we shall find out about in this chapter.

2) HELPING AN EXCLUDED PERSON FIT IN BETTER WITH A GROUP

You might occasionally witness a scene at work or when you go out, where an unfortunate individual is shut out from the rest of the group. They may be shy or have physical features which induce discriminatory reactions in others. Whatever the cause, you notice their isolation and uneasiness.

The number one problem is that most people confronted with this situation feel helpless and embarrassed, not knowing what to do. More often than not, they pretend not to see the excluded person and carry on chatting cheerfully with their colleagues!

This is an extremely delicate state of affairs to manage, as we are at a loss to know what to say to this person at the risk of making them feel even more uncomfortable in public. Yet, it is better to fumble about and say a few considerate words rather than completely ignoring the isolated individual. The reason for this is that we must realise exclusion is the worst thing a human being can experience. It can lead to depression and isolation.

Put yourself in their shoes. Imagine that you are in a group of eight people. You notice that everyone is talking amongst themselves and deliberately ignoring you. At the end of the day, upon your return home, you would feel in a very bad way, demoralised, ashamed, with negative thoughts recurring over several days. This is a reality one should not underestimate. However, a few kind words from someone during that social gathering would have done you a lot of good and been a 'lifesaver', maintaining a feeling of hope within you.

Here are the rules to follow when dealing with an excluded person:

♦ First of all, it is perfectly normal and understandable for you to feel powerless to do anything about the other person's unease. It is not your fault! However, pretending not to see them or ignoring them is not the right approach. It is always best to show them signs of availability: eye contact, smiling, friendly approaches…

♦ Behave in a normal sociable manner just as you would with others. There is no point in having an overly compassionate attitude. This is the best way to show respect to that person.

♦ Use **inclusive phrases** to help them take part in the conversation. Use a sentence or a discreet question such as the following:

"And how about you?" "And you, what are your interests in life?" "Do you agree with what's been said?" "What's your opinion?" "What sort of activity would you enjoy doing?" "Would you like to have a coffee with us?" "Would you like another drink?" And so on.

It is up to you to find the right question with regard to the context. You simply show the person that they exist and that is the main thing. Avoid doing it too often, every three minutes, for example. Space out your questions. Just ask them from time to time so as not to appear intrusive.

♦ If the other person reacts badly (unease, silence, haughty attitude) – and unfortunately this can happen – remind yourself that it could be an instinctively protective reaction. Do not take it personally. When a person is focused on their discontent, they may no longer heed social codes. Rest assured that, generally speaking, the excluded person will be touched by your concern and respond to you in a courteous way.

♦ Lastly, and this is the most important thing to remember. These small tokens of attention are frequently enough to give reticent people the confidence they need to make an effort to mix in and take part in the conversation. They probably would have done nothing at all and stayed in their little corner had you not proffered them a helping hand. We must try to give them a helping hand without forcing them to open up to you completely.

If the person continues shutting him or herself out on purpose in spite of your efforts, you will be unable to try to help them anymore. They have the right to withdraw and we must respect their decision. Some people prefer to be left alone. Others, being the majority, want to fit in better and are simply looking for a bit of help. Perhaps they are shy or wary to begin with and need time to become acquainted with the group to feel more at ease.

Whatever the outcome, you will have nothing to regret – as a kindly human being, you will have done your bit.

HOW TO HELP AN EXCLUDED PERSON FIT IN WITH A GROUP

IGNORE HIM OR
HELP HIM OUT A LITTLE?

SIMPLE, KINDLY ACTIONS:

1) Approach the person

2) Use an inclusive phrase
E.g. "Would you like to come and have a chat with us?"
E.g. "Would you like to have a coffee with us?"

3) Give them openings to encourage them to speak
E.g. "Do you agree with what's being said?"
E.g. "How about you, what did you do this weekend?"

It only takes a few seconds to help a person mix in better. Then, they're free to play the social game or not, but you will have done YOUR BIT.

The ideal society would be one in which there was not the slightest exclusion, but obviously that society would be utopian! We cannot help everybody to fit in better or fight against every form of discrimination! This is because it is a highly complex societal subject dependent on so many different factors, such as individual human cases, corporate habits and customs, community life, and so forth.

When you go out, you might sometimes come across people with a more serious disability (autism, hearing impairment, paralysis, etc.). It is human and normal not to know how to react to people with problems which we are not used to encountering on a daily basis. Occasionally, in the work environment you might also have to contend with awkward personalities (a paranoid person, an obsessive character, a narcissist…) who adversely affect team spirit. These are tricky situations to handle. They require tact and diplomacy.

It is not your role to resolve all these issues or to try to help everyone fit in. Just play your part – that is the lesson to assimilate from this chapter. Be active rather than passive. A few friendly words are better than silence or condescension.

Whether you are at a party or at work, a few words or a straightforward human gesture can make all the difference and help achieve more social harmony around you.

3) HELPING OTHERS FIT IN BETTER WITH A GROUP

Now then, let us imagine a different situation: *you* are the person who is excluded from the group and you do not know what to do to fit in better. You have tremendous difficulty because of your disability or some distinctive characteristic. You want people to get the message that they should be helping you, or reaching out to you.

When people are ignoring and isolating you, their behaviour is not conducive to your making efforts to fit in. Obviously, the best solution – and the one recommended by this book – is to take the bull by the horns and make the first move. In this way, you make other people's work easier.

For example:

> ➢ **Say a few sentences to initiate conversation with them. This forces people to interact and pay attention to you.**

> ➢ **Use Available Social Communication (ASC) to keep connecting with them, even if you carry on being shy or reserved.**

Despite this, the situation may continue to be tense and very awkward. Either members of the group will feel uncomfortable with your disability and not dare to chat with you, or you will be the one to feel distraught and not know what to do to fit in. This is especially so over the long term with people you have to see regularly, such as those at work.

As a last resort, a solution might also be forthcoming from other people – there is a real chance things will be easier if they do help us out a bit. It is always possible to help people help you!

The first thing to do is to try to understand their feeling of helplessness. They see everything from afar. They do not necessarily comprehend your unease. They just find your attitude curious and might interpret your silence as a lack of interest in their group. They do not know what to do and so remain passive.

There are not all that many remedies. The best thing for you is to seize the initiative and attempt to reassure your colleagues about your predicament by being open with them. Let them know about your disability or distinctive characteristics in a few sentences as being the cause of your seemingly aloof behaviour towards them.

Example 1: *"Forgive me if I seem to have difficulties once in a while. In fact, I have a slight disability: I have hearing problems. I find it hard to hear and I need people to repeat things sometimes. But I can assure you that I will then understand perfectly (smile)! Feel free to ask how to go about talking to me because I know it's not easy for you. I won't be offended (smile)!"*

Example 2: *"In fact, I tend to be a very reserved sort of person. Sometimes, I'm not very talkative. But let me assure you that I'm still here (smile) and pleased to be with you. Feel free to help me out a bit and reach out to me when you see me having difficulty because it helps me fit in better."*

This advice might seem counter-intuitive because the usual recommendation is to adjust to others and learn how to hide one's vulnerabilities. Only apply it as a last resort and if you feel the situation requires it! Nevertheless, introducing yourself in this way is not without its benefits:

♦ Within a few minutes, other people will get to know you and gain a better understanding of your attitude towards them in the group. Let us not forget that they see us from a distance and giving them a few explanations will help put their mind at ease.

♦ The most important thing is to say it with a smile – show that you are comfortable with your disability. Play down the situation. People will respect you more and feel more at ease with you.

♦ Feel free to give a few instructions so they understand that they should help you out from time to time. This can be seen as a true effort to fit in on your part. People are bound to appreciate that.

♦ Sincere, heartfelt communication always remains the most appealing way to make contact. It spurs people into making an effort to put themselves in your shoes. Sincerity can resolve many a problem in just a few moments, whilst feigning sincerity can prolong problems for life without ever resolving them!

♦ Above all, as far as you are concerned, you will feel more comfortable on a day-to-day basis with your colleagues and friends. You will no longer feel compelled to play a role all the time or feel the pressure of other people's perception of you. You have come to terms with your distinctive characteristics and people realise that. You will be more at peace with yourself and others which is fundamental to your well-being.

These tips will not definitively guarantee successful mixing in but at least they have the merit of seeking to include rather than exclude you. They suggest potential ways of achieving better harmony between you and your colleagues. This might succeed or fail. Everything depends on your situation, the nature of your disability, the kindliness of people around you, and your way of presenting things…

HOW TO FIT IN WITH A GROUP
WHEN YOU ARE EXCLUDED

THREE POTENTIAL SOLUTIONS:

1) I make the first move
E.g. I approach the other person; I start up a conversation...

2) Use Available Social Communication
E.g. I remain reserved within the group, but I smile, agree, and appear available, etc.

3) Help others to welcome me into the group
▶ I explain, I reassure people about my disability or personality.
▶ I keep up a sincere, straightforward and smiling demeanour.
▶ I give a few instructions to help them.

"Sometimes people don't know what to do in response to your silence – you need to help them help you."

CHAPTER XIII

HELPING A SHY CHILD MAKE FRIENDS

All the advice given up to this point has generally applied to the realm of adults. Obviously, some of the tips cannot be adapted for children, such as those in the previous chapter on fitting in with a group. Other advice, however, remains applicable, as we shall see.

The subject of childhood is far more complex. It deserves an entire book to expand on the topic and take into account all the specific situations a shy teenager may encounter when experiencing difficulties making friends or fitting in at school.

Although this chapter may seem non-exhaustive in light of the magnitude of the subject, we shall nevertheless try to compile the most relevant solutions. These are to help parents who have an introverted child and do not always know how to help him or her through their difficulties. At some time or another in your married or family life, you will no doubt bring up a child. Perhaps your son or daughter will be shy like you. It is always a good thing to know the ABC of social communication for children and teenagers. Then, you will be better able to cope with these problems should they occur.

Lets us imagine the following real-life situation:

Your child, Tom, 8, is very shy. When you have guests round at the house, he immediately takes refuge in his bedroom. When there are invitations to go out, either he will refuse to come or when he does go to a family celebration he will remain wordless in a corner all evening. He does not play with other children at school. He is anxious and does not speak in class.

You notice that his shyness is adversely affecting his development. You start to get worried and would like to help bring him out of his shyness and make a few friends…

Here are the Six Principles to remember in order to help your shy child

♦ **Firstly, accept his or her individuality.**
To begin with, you have to accept his or her personality. Above all, avoid making your child feel guilty about their shyness and telling them

they are abnormal. Otherwise, they will feel yet more ill-at-ease. Quite the reverse, explain to him or her that they are just different. Tell them, for instance, that you were like them when you were a child and that, with time, you managed to overcome your shyness.

♦ **Give him or her confidence and love.**
More than anything, a child who has poor self-esteem needs confidence and emotional support if they are to learn how to overcome their mental blocks. If you do not encourage them, they might give up. Positive words, compliments and morale-boosting have the effect of stimulating the child into making an effort to tackle any difficulties arising from their shyness.

♦ **Explain to him or her that action and habit alleviate anxiety.**
This is the principle of 'gradual exposure'. If your child is afraid to go to his or her first music lesson, tell them it is perfectly normal to feel nervous the first time. They will feel much more relaxed at the second lesson and then even better by the third. With habit, any fear will disappear. Prove it to them by reminding them of any of their previous positive experiences.

♦ **Encourage him or her to open up to others.**
Reassure them and encourage them to approach others rather than cutting themselves off. Tell him or her that other kids are nice but can sometimes be mocking because they do not know what it means to be different. With time, they will end up accepting you better. Concentrate on the benefits: he or she can make new friends, learn new things, discover new games, and so on.

♦ **Find stimulating activities.**
As is said throughout this book, having interests and leisure pursuits makes it easier to connect with people. The same goes for children. If you find some activities they really enjoy, it will be much easier to motivate them into opening up to other people and making friends. Sport, music, IT or arts – find a pursuit which they might enjoy – there have to be some. Join your child up to a club and give him or her permission to invite friends over at the weekend to share in a leisure activity.

♦ **Teach him or her Available Social Communication (ASC).**
If your child is anxious and afraid of not knowing what to say at family gatherings or parties with guests, reassure him or her by explaining that there is no need to talk a great deal, just learn how to appear available

and cheerful. All that is needed are a few little routines to use in a group context. This will take a lot of pressure off a child.

Practical, fun tools to help your shy child

It is quite understandable that a parent might still find it hard to help their child despite the potential solutions provided. What differs as compared with the realm of adults is that children are more spontaneous and react depending on their impulses and level of affectivity. At that age, they do not yet have the maturity required and have not assimilated the values essential for understanding self-discipline and the sense of effort. So, have no hesitation in using innovative games and fun resources to inspire them. We have detailed a few ideas below.

♦ **The game of the confidence-building shining sun.**
Get your child to draw a wonderful sun in yellow felt-tip with a dozen rays around it. On each of the rays, he or she has to write in black pen one of their positive attributes: joyful, generous, intelligent, patient, curious, kind, funny, imaginative, etc.

In this way, they will see a sun shining with all their good points. When they see this as a picture, they will be much better able to visualise and understand what they can offer others. They can hang it up in their bedroom as a reminder whenever they need it.

♦ **Keep a success log: "Today, I managed to…"**
Saying "hello" to a stranger, speaking in front of a group and going to a festive event are all actions which can require a lot of effort from an anxious child. It is beneficial for the child to visualise and celebrate his or her progress by using a book to note down the successes of the day. They will become very proud of it and this will encourage them to keep up their efforts!

♦ **Fun breathing and relaxation techniques.**
Meditation, deep breathing and yoga can help your child manage anxiety-provoking situations. This they can do in their bedroom or after getting up and have fun reproducing yoga positions, such as the frog, koala and camel poses or sun salutations, and so on. There are various Internet resources which provide dozens of different fun poses to do, such as those shown in the book, *Yoga for Children: 200+ Yoga Poses* by Lisa Flynn.

♦ **Appoint him or her to be "boss" or play-act shyness with them.**
The idea is to encourage the child into taking action themselves in order to learn how to overcome their fears. You can appoint them to be "boss," to do the shopping, or organise the schedule of a family outing...
You can also play-act with them. If you are lost in town and you are looking for their toyshop, pretend to be searching for a map in your bag and tell him or her that you cannot find it. Another example: when you are at the cinema, the person next to you will have to move over a seat so that you three (mum, dad and child) can all sit down together. You tell your child that you dare not ask the person to move over and that is a shame. You will be surprised to see how eagerly they will ask the person themselves.

♦ **Keep a friendship log.**
When a child is shy, they tend to withdraw and avoid others. If you keep a friendship log, they will be pleased to see all the new friends they have made and this will spur them on to be more forthcoming with people. In the log, the child can write down on each page their new friend's first name, add their photo, note down what they like about the friend, the excursions they have gone on together, and the two favourite things he or she remembers doing with them... With a friendship log, the child can better visualise the benefits of reaching out to others.

♦ **Play out social situations with soft toys.**
You take soft toys and enact the social situations of everyday life with your child. For example, you play at being a soft toy which is alone in the playground, looking from a distance at another child playing marbles. Your child has to take part in the scene and help the 'shy toy' connect with the other child so that they can play together. To do this, he or she must learn how to use signs of sociability.

♦ **Create a motivation chart with rewards.**
Every week, you can suggest a few little challenges to your child to help him or her conquer shyness. For instance, saying 'hello' and smiling at a guest who has come to the house; paying a compliment to a friend; speaking up in class; going over to the canteen table where other children are sitting, and eating with them, etc.
The child can hang the chart up in their bedroom and when they have reached their goals, they will deserve a reward! Be careful! The idea is to find healthy objectives to aid your child in surmounting their timidity in a way which is gentle, and not force them to do anything against their will.

CHAPTER XIV

SEEKING SOCIAL HARMONY

WHY DOES IT WORK IN SOME CULTURES?

At a time when our modern society places more of an emphasis on the individual and his or her independence (success, critical thinking, freedom, their appearance, and so on), it is good to remind ourselves that some traditional societies (although not denying the concept of the individual) did focus more on the values of the collective (the community, authority, rites, etc.).

The pre-eminence of the collective over the individual results in different social structures in which the influence of the solidarity is greater and no deviation from the norm is tolerated. Furthermore, in villages we used to see the same people regularly. We encountered problems and resolved them together. In modern society with the expansion of cities, independence and personal liberties are encouraged instead.

It is not a question of proclaiming which society is better as each model has both its advantages and drawbacks. One has to adapt to the society in which one lives! The goal is to gain a better understanding and draw inspiration from it in order to pick out the best aspects.

	TRADITIONAL SOCIETY	**MODERN SOCIETY**
Dominating values	Community, religion, group rules, authority, solidarity, faith, family	Freedom, success, reason, independence, one's image, happiness, individual rights
Primary focus	*Social harmony*	*Individual harmony*
Consequences on friendship and social life	People live within a community; relationships are stronger and common goals are shared	It's harder to establish and maintain a true relationship because "each person does their own thing"

> ⇨ To maintain relationships today, it might be helpful to go back to certain values or routines and find <u>common goals</u> to share with other people.

Modern societies are characterised by their obsession with prioritising the life of the individual: how to be happy, choose the best career path, find one's ideal apartment, satisfy one's impulses and desires within a consumer society, and so on.

However, if we falter on this path of individuality, we risk comparing ourselves with others and being faced with isolation and depression.

In traditional societies, we did not necessarily care about any of this because the individual was not 'king' and had to submit to the rules of the community, the chief or a God.

Personal whims were not put first; rather faith and community life took precedence over individual well-being. The search for social cohesion remained the priority.

Therefore, in our everyday lives, we can get inspiration from some traditional cultures or philosophies which advocate a particular concept of social harmony. Certain maxims might appeal to you and encourage you to consider others more. Some quotations include the following:

Ubuntu (African concept)	*"I am because we are."* That is to say, other people also contribute to our identity. We only fully exist when we share with others and relate to them.
The Christian Bible	*"Do unto others as you would they do unto you."* (Luke 6:31)
Ayni (amongst the Quechuas)	*"What I do for you today, you will do for me tomorrow."* This concept means reciprocity; a system of mutual support enabling communities of American Indians to survive without money and exchange services between each other.

Ren (Chinese concept)	仁: The Chinese character is comprised of two components "man" and "two." Ren is essentially a concept to do with relationships and means *benevolence*, something which must guide every human in their interactions with others.

RESPECT FOR RITUALS:
THE SOLUTION PRODUCING SOCIAL HARMONY?

How is it possible to live in peace with others when we are surrounded by hundreds of human beings at work or school? Does a universal theory exist which could offer the key to social harmony in any human community? These are the fascinating questions which Confucius had already attempted to answer in the Fifth Century B.C.

The renowned Chinese philosopher recommended practising *Ren* with human beings. It is a benevolent, virtuous attitude based on respect for rituals (*Li*). That is to say, it is a collection of rules of behaviour and proprieties guiding good relations between individuals.

This is because, in order to live in harmony with others, there has to be a system of codes and values which an individual must respect when interacting with their fellow humans. It is akin to a score of musical notes which each person in an orchestra must play so that everything is in tune. There is a certain way to behave. If raising a hand and smiling to greet someone are required, then that ritual must be respected. A nice gesture and a kind word are lovely 'chords'. The realm of rituals is a musical one. Every human being is sensitive to a beautiful chord and responds accordingly. If the notes are badly played, there will be discord and dysfunction within a relationship.

Confucius added that feelings have to be restored because when they accompany our words, they make our actions sincere and still nobler. It just so happens that what principally differentiates man from animals is empathy.

As the individual has this extraordinary ability to put him or herself in someone else's place, they might as well use it and extend it to their social network of family, friends and colleagues. Thus, the world would be a better place and there would be more social harmony. Nevertheless, too much benevolence leads to excess and some people may take advantage of it. Too much severity leads to injustice. The solution is to aim for a happy medium.

There is a world of rituals and in order to live in harmony with others people must comply. The direct application of the theories of Confucius in the real lives of every family in China is testament to this. Loving one's parents, respecting ancestors along with obeying one's superiors and elders all guarantee good political organisation and social cohesion. Without rituals, disorder and disrespect prevail within families.

For example, there are rituals and ceremonies practised by millions of Chinese where, with incense sticks in hand, offerings of food are made to the Gods and ancestors. There is great respect for our parents who brought us into the world. We take care of them until they pass on. Education of children is also a question of honour. There is emphasis on the values of discipline and success.

The word harmony (和) carries a lot of significance and is highly fashionable in China, where folk are constantly looking for harmony between people and with nature. Many Westerners are amazed at the importance of the family in Chinese life. By now, you will have understood that all this derives from the heritage of Confucius and the impact of rituals.

Confucian thought is at the heart of our book which sets out to show that there is no need to scale mountains or change one's personality simply to live in harmony with others. Applying a few little routines is often enough to improve a relationship and mix in with others.

Ultimately, human relations are like a piece of music. The harmony of your relationship with others and the entire community depends on that collection of intermingling 'sounds' and gestures.

PRACTICAL INFO SHEETS

"Nature needs to be worked on."
Paul Valéry

"Knowing is not enough, we must also implement;
wanting is not enough, we must also take action."
Goethe

Important:

• Carefully reread these info sheets every time you feel the need in your life. They have been formulated to assist you in your work on yourself and on your social communication.

• These info sheets are brimming with inspirational solutions and can provide valuable support to help you resolve a variety of everyday social situations.

• Although ready-made phrases might seem contrived, they do actually serve to guide with practical examples those people most in difficulty, socially.

INFO SHEET 1

EYE CONTACT

Eye contact is the first means of communication between two people. It shows that you want to interact with the other person.

Even if you look at someone from far away, eye contact can be "an act which has an effect at a distance" which indicates that you are paying close attention to that person.

Avoiding someone's gaze, looking away and lowering your eyes may be signs that you do not wish to interact with the person to whom you are talking or that you are ill at ease.

When someone is speaking, they look at the other person (41% of the time) which is less than when they are listening to him or her (75% of the time).[18]

A steady gaze is a sign of attention showing that you are engaged in the conversation with the other person and are genuinely listening.

So, to look at someone is to communicate. Wherever you go, it is essential to look at people in the eye if you want to connect with them.

Glancing at someone in a shopping centre or café is enough to start an interaction – think about that!

Social interactions are usually interspersed with brief moments of visual contact lasting a few mini-seconds.

However, when we start to stare at a person, this may create a sense of uneasiness in them.

The length of eye contact can indicate how close your relationship with a person is.

You hold eye contact longer with your mother or spouse. By contrast, your eye contact with a stranger is fleeting.

Accordingly, eye contact promotes relationships and closeness.

For some people, looking at a person in the eye can be difficult...
especially with strangers!

SOME HELPFUL TIPS

● Focus on one eye only and then alternate:
Instead of looking at both eyes at the same time, it will help you if you focus on one eye only and then switch from one eye to the other every 10 seconds.

● Find another point on the face where you can focus your gaze:
If you are intimidated by the other person's eyes, look instead at the bridge of their nose, an eyebrow or just below the eye. Do this discreetly.

● When you lower your gaze, accompany this action with a gesture:
If you feel uneasy as you look away, accompany your action with a natural movement, such as nodding your head, smiling or shifting your position...

● Make yourself look into the person's eyes and concentrate on what they are saying:
The best way is always to look people in the eye and maintain visual contact while you are speaking or listening. Relax and concentrate on what the person is saying to you at that moment.

● Practise at home, in front of a mirror, or on the tube (subway):
If you are still finding it difficult, practise at home in front of a mirror or with pictures or videos of people looking in your direction. Train yourself in the street or on the tube. Look at people in the eye but avoid staring at them!

INFO SHEET 2

SMILING

A smile is the most demonstrative sign of sociability there is. When you see a person smile at you, it is enough to make you want to interact with them straightaway and put you in a good mood.

The most effective way to make friends easily is to start off with a smile. Whether you are a reserved or shy person, a sincere smile from the heart shows that you WANT to interact with people.

Smiling changes your state of mind and requires little effort. Everyone can do it. Even a pessimistic person knows how to give a warm smile at least once during the course of a meeting.

As the Chinese proverb goes, "Smile three times a day and you won't need any medicine."

Indeed, smiling leads to the release of endorphins (the hormones which cause the feeling of well-being) and lowers the level of cortisol (the stress-related hormone).[19]

Smiling for a few seconds puts you almost instantaneously into a sociable, happier frame of mind. Above all, smiling promotes friendship; it is 'contagious' and encourages people to smile back at you.

As Abbé Pierre used to say, "A smile costs less than electricity but gives just as much light."

Reflect on this: When you want a person to take an interest in you or to notice you in a room, start by giving them a smile. It is effective – it will lead to the person coming over to you and engaging you in conversation.

For some people, smiling can be difficult... especially at strangers!

SOME HELPFUL TIPS

● **Think happy thoughts:**
It is hard to smile if you are a pessimistic person. However, it will help you if you think of a line or scene from a film which you find amusing, or a loved one or a memory from your life which fills you with happiness. Think carefully, there must be something!

- **In your mind's eye, picture a radiant smile on a person's face:**
Before approaching a person, imagine there is a warm smile already on their face lighting it up like bright sunshine. Visualise this wonderful, welcoming smile on their face. This will encourage you to make contact with other people with a smile.

- **Identify the source of your problem:**
The idea is to feel comfortable with your smile, understand the causes of any issue (e.g., stained teeth) and find a suitable solution (e.g., teeth whitening). Alternatively, the reason might be that you do not like people, so it will help you if you change your state of mind and focus on positive opportunities (such as a new friend, rewarding conversations which may do you good, and so on).

- **Think of other things to make you smile:**
A play on words (The duck said to the barman, "Put it on my bill!"); role-playing (the first one to smile wins); humorous music (Ordinary Average Guy – Joe Walsh), the sound of your baby laughing, etc.

- **Train yourself to smile naturally by doing exercises:**
Smiling does not come naturally to some people but things can really click into place for them by carrying out a few practical exercises. See the two examples just below.

PRACTICAL APPLICATION No. 1: Set yourself the target of smiling at five people throughout the day. You will be pleasantly surprised at people's reaction. You are not only conveying a good mood but you are also encouraging people to smile back at you and, most importantly, interact with you, or even get closer to you. In the end, everyone is a winner.

PRACTICAL APPLICATION No. 2: Do the following test at work, for example. Spend a normal day in which you interact with your colleagues or customers as usual.

The next day, interact with people but this time with a real winning smile on your face. Smile sincerely as you say "hello" to them and see the difference it makes to their reaction. You will observe that a smile is powerful and is enough to change people.

These two exercises should convince you how important smiling is in your social communication. You are not obliged to smile permanently if this is not in your character but a simple warm smile might help you improve your interactions and make forming relationships easier – that is the key point to remember.

INFO SHEET 3

USING PHYSICAL CONTACT
TO HELP FORM A RELATIONSHIP

In the same way as eye contact and smiling, physical gestures are part of non-verbal communication. Speaking with gestures, tapping someone on the shoulder and shaking somebody's hand all express one's sincere wish to interact with that person.

Some gestures may have more impact than words in helping build relationships. For example, a friendly and forthright hug can say a lot more in a few seconds than a long speech – think about that!

What is more, gestures have a universal reach. If you nod your head and smile or give a thumbs-up as a sign of approval, most people will swiftly grasp your message.

It is well-known that 'form' (gestures, facial expressions, the voice) is far more crucial in making a good impression on people than 'substance' (i.e., the content of conversation).

At the end of a meeting, the person you have been talking to is more likely to recall your smile, the emotion in your voice, and your cordial gestures than the words you have spoken.

That is why in everyday life, it is important to know how to use the body to express oneself in order to interact with people successfully.

Furthermore, various scientific experiments[20] conducted by research psychologists have shown that tactile contact has a positive, significant influence on our social interactions. You are bound to have already heard about the following sort of anecdote: experiments carried out in the school environment which demonstrate that a mere touch from a teacher on a student's shoulder increased his/her obedience and concentration; or in the sales or restaurant industry, that minor tactile contact between a salesperson and their customer was enough to increase their chances of making a sale or receiving a better tip.

How can these findings be explained? Quite simply, it is because touch is a sign of attention. It creates a feeling of being close to the person who is then more willing to put his or her trust in someone.

This is confirmed by another famous experiment.[21] A student deliberately leaves some coins in a telephone box and then goes back to ask the person who has gone in next whether they have found any money. The student gets a 96% affirmative answer rate when physical contact is involved (for instance, a light touch on the forearm). This is as compared with only 63% when there is no physical contact, and people lie, denying that they have seen any money. Likewise, with a similar experiment in the street, we find that 29% of people agree to give a little money to a stranger to help him out, with this proportion rising to 51% if the stranger touches them briefly. These figures are most significant and indicative of the impact which touch has in social interactions.

---

4 TIPS TO REMEMBER

● **Limit self-touch gestures:**
Self-touch gestures (rubbing your forehead, holding your chin, scratching your nose, etc.) are introverted gestures. During meetings, they are to be avoided in so far as is possible.

● **Opt for open gestures:**
Closed gestures or ones which point downwards (crossed arms, clenched fist with the thumb pointing downwards) are negative signifiers. Open gestures or ones which point upwards (open arms, clenched fist with the thumb pointing upwards) usually deliver a positive message and encourage interaction.

● **Use bonding gestures to get closer to people**:
There are powerful gestures which will hasten bonding, such as a hug, a friendly tap on the shoulder, arms outstretched to the other person, and so on.

● **Physical contact makes a real difference:**
Touching is a sign of attention. When you use tactile contact, it can add a warmer, more human aspect to your interactions. Example: when you shake someone's hand, remember to touch their forearm with the other hand. If you kiss them on the cheek, touch their hip at the same time with one of your hands.

INFO SHEET 4

KNOWING HOW TO HOLD
A CONVERSATION

Conversation is the main means of communication between individuals. It largely determines the length of a social interaction. When people have nothing more to say to each other, they part company.

So, for those who find it hard to hold a conversation, such as shy or introverted people, meetings can be a real ordeal because they live in constant fear of not knowing what to say and have to face "going blank."

In this info sheet, we shall go through some practical tips to help you hold a conversation and handle those "blanks" better.

First of all, conversational content is generally dominated by what we call "small talk." That is to say, casual conversation where you speak about everything and nothing of significance, such as daily, trivial occurrences, without there necessarily being any purpose to it!

Although small talk remains superficial, it is essential in order to connect with others, inasmuch as people often prefer to talk about down-to-earth things, such as the weather, cooking and the news, before getting into more personal subjects.

For introverted people, small talk can be a rather tedious ordeal because they usually prefer talking about deeper and more personal topics. However, it is a stage which has to be got through before one can get involved in more rewarding discussions.

To help you find topics of conversation easily during a meeting, there are plenty of little things around you which can give you ideas:

1) **Your surroundings:**
The gorgeous or gloomy weather today; the atmosphere of the café where you are having a drink; the mood of people around you; the appearance of the person you are talking to; nice places to visit in town, and so on.

2) **The news:**
The latest important political events; the TV schedule for this evening or yesterday; cultural news; the latest films in the cinema; the YouTube

video everyone is talking about at the moment; the latest celebrity interview in a magazine, etc.

3) My personal situation or the situation of the person to whom you are talking:
Work; current leisure pursuits; family life; last or next weekend's activities, etc.

As you can see, there are masses of potential topics which can keep a conversation going and get someone to talk!

However, if that little chat is starting to bore you... to get out of it, the best solution is always to REDIRECT it towards your favourite topics of conversation and talk about things which matter to you.

For example, talk about your interests or those which may appeal to the other person:

- Your favourite sport
- The TV series you watch the most
- Your latest trips
- Your observations on the differences between men and women
- Your strange passion for plants

If you deeply dislike a conversation and you are having to endure it, there are only two possible solutions:

● Either you try to save face and remain reserved and courteous, adopting available social communication (A.S.C.).

● Or, you subtly switch the topic of conversation and introduce subjects which do matter to you:
"By the way, do you happen to have heard about..." or *"You know, at the moment, I..."*

For as long as you do not intervene, the discussion taking place will progress in the way that the other person wants!

You can see it for yourself in everyday life. When a topic of discussion suddenly changes, it is because one of our friends has started to talk about something else, although there might be no connection between the previous and following subjects – isn't that so?

Therefore, it is important to take the initiative so that you learn how to influence a discussion.

THE ART OF CONVERSATION: POINTS TO REMEMBER

✓ The form (i.e., the outward approach, expressiveness and manner) is more important than the substance (the content, verbal discourse).

✓ Small talk is an essential step to be able to progress to deeper subjects.

✓ Do listen attentively to the other person in order to bounce off such valuable information as he or she gives you.

✓ Combine ideas to enhance the discussion: start off with an initial topic and bring in more personal anecdotes: *"Hey, that reminds me of..."*

✓ The more you take the initiative in conversations, the more the conversation's content will be in line with your personal wishes.

Six practical tips to handle going blank in a conversation:

✓ Repeat the other person's last words or summarise their words for as long as it takes you to find inspiration:
"Mmm... yes, you mean that Mark preferred to go to the cinema..."

✓ Ask open-ended questions to get the other person to talk:
"By the way, what do you think about...?" or *"What makes you say that?"* and so on.

✓ Use stepping stone formulations to encourage him or her to go further:
"What do you mean?" "And then?" "Never!" "Is that so?" "Oh, really?" "Can you be more precise?" etc.

✓ If you feel awkward, appear to be thinking about what the other person has just said to justify your silence.

✓ Use the expression *"That reminds me"* to interject an anecdote:
"What you say there reminds me of a trip I went on when I was in the South..."

✓ Go back to a previous topic of conversation if the current discussion has petered out:
"Anyway, you were saying to me a few minutes ago..."

As we have seen, conversational content is dominated primarily by small talk, but fortunately it is not limited to this, otherwise discussions between people would remain dull. To have a successful conversation, other, more personal information about oneself and the other person, needs to be added.

Hence, if we were to give rough estimate to get an idea of the right balance, a good conversation would consist of:

30% talking about oneself; 30% taking an interest in the other person; and 40% trivial discussion.

In the next few Info Sheets, we shall learn how to speak about oneself and take an interest in the other person – two prerequisites for making our conversations a success!

INFO SHEET 5

LEARNING TO TALK ABOUT YOURSELF

Talking about yourself is an act of social communication which is used to present your personality. It makes it possible for the other person to tell who you really are and get to know your personal character: your status, tastes and leisure activities.

If you never talk about yourself when you interact with other people, then it is likely that they will talk mostly about themselves and never get to know you.

Talking about yourself is important too because you not only provide people with hints about your personal status but also give them the opportunity to proffer you openings to nurture a conversation. For instance, *"By the way, how's your girlfriend?" "How are your guitar lessons going?" "Have you sorted out those problems you were having?"* are all things your work colleague might ask you, to initiate a conversation when he meets you in the corridor...

If you do not give any clues about yourself, then you will remain something of a mystery to him or her, and it will be hard to build a deep, genuine relationship.

You risk being affected by this because you might appear too neutral and unassuming as you deal with each situation.

Whether you are at work or out and about, be sure to talk a little about yourself. This helps assert your character and make your conversations more personal.

Nevertheless, it is true that some bashful people experience great difficulty talking about themselves. Either they keep the conversation going with a few light anecdotes and flashes of humour, or they ask the other person too many questions by getting them to talk about themselves. Such individuals do everything they can to make sure the discussion does not revolve around them!

We suggest various solutions below for learning how to talk about oneself:

<u>1st Practical Solution</u>: **Identify the reasons for your mental blocks and accept yourself.**

The deep-seated difficulties you have in talking about yourself may be associated with any of the following:

- Reticence.

- Your upbringing; your culture.

- Personal traumas which prevent you from being yourself.

- Poor self-esteem; fear of being judged by the other person.

ACTION! Think very carefully. Understanding the reasons may be enough to reduce certain mental blocks and provide appropriate solutions. In any event, it is vital that you accept yourself as you are with your qualities and shortcomings in order to be able to talk about yourself with complete sincerity.

<u>2nd Practical Solution</u>: **Make regular use of the personal pronoun "I"**

Instead of using the personal pronoun "you" as you normally would to get other people to talk, push yourself into conversations by starting your sentences with "I."

Examples:

I feel…
I'd like to talk to you about...
As for me, I'd say...
I need...

ACTION! In every single encounter (not just from time to time!), remember to apply this method of using the personal pronoun "I" because it is the only way to conquer your reticence and make real progress.

<u>3rd Practical Solution</u>: **Speak about your interests and plus points**

There are three broad topics of discussion which highlight your personality, allowing people to get to know you properly:

- *My areas of interest and leisure activities:* 1) .... 2) .... 3) ....

- *My lifelong aspirations:* 1) .... 2) .... 3) ......

- *My personal qualities; my values:* 1) .... 2) .... 3) ....

ACTION! Write your answers down on a piece of paper if you need to get things straight in your mind. In between lightweight banter over the course of a meeting, deliberately try to insert these conversational topics and talk as much as possible about them whilst remaining attentive to what the other person is saying.

Examples: *"You know, one of my interests is..." "At the weekend, I go to..." I'm an idealistic sort of person because..." "People say I have a lot of imagination because..." "One day, I'd like to..."*

4th Practical Solution: **Use the storytelling technique**

We all have a little story to tell others which could sum up our life. This biographical account can be based on encounters, trips, life lessons, or personal struggles which we have won. Even though our life might not necessarily be brimming with positive events, there are definitely fascinating things to share. What is the point of storytelling? The story compels you to disclose yourself honestly to others.

So, ask yourself these questions: *"What is my story? What could I recount so that others get to know me better?"*

Examples: *"I grew up in a family of..." "I lived through the..." "I met my first..." "My character probably stems from that time when..." "I recall..." "One life lesson I'll never forget is..."*

ACTION! At a meeting, set yourself the goal of holding a five to ten-minute monologue to present your personal story; your background. Storytelling always makes a good impression and has the power to make the person who uses it likeable and endearing.

If you follow these tips and implement them diligently every time you go out, you will see that they really work and people will get to know you better!

INFO SHEET 6

HOW TO TAKE A GENUINE INTEREST IN OTHER PEOPLE

A discussion between two people is interactive. It is healthy when the speaker manages to find a balance between talking about him or herself and genuinely taking an interest in the other person.

A person who only holds monologues telling everyone about their life and talking about humdrum everyday occurrences will swiftly bore the person to whom they are talking. There is also a need to know how to take an interest in the other person and try to understand them better!

What purpose does it serve to take an interest in the other person during a conversation?

- To get to know the person truly.

- To build a deeper relationship; to connect.

- To show one's interest in the person. Who is not flattered when someone takes a genuine interest in them?

Dale Carnegie once famously said: *"You can make more friends in two months by becoming interested in other people than you can in two years by trying to get other people interested in you."*

Nevertheless, for some people, taking an interest in others does not come as easily and naturally as suggested because one does not dare to, or one does not necessarily know how to go about it!

So, here is a collection of tips to help you take an interest in the other person during a conversation:

1st Practical Solution: **Ask questions**

Obviously, the first (and most effective!) way to get to know the person you are talking to is to ask questions. If you do not do this, then you have very little chance of really getting to know to whom you are speaking.

ACTION! During a discussion, pluck up the courage to ask simple but more personal questions if you want the person to reveal more about themselves. Opt for *open-ended questions* so that they do not just answer with a yes or no. Examples: *"What are your interests?" "Did you do anything special this weekend?" "Can you tell me a bit more about your projects?" "What attracts you to this job?"*

2nd Practical Solution: **Become an active listener**

We often tend to talk, recounting lots of anecdotes, interrupting other people, and do not realise that we are not listening to the person in front of us. There is a quotation by Epictetus which says, *"We have two ears and one mouth so that we can listen twice as much as we speak."*

Listening involves being quiet from time to time so that we can genuinely pay attention to the other person – to take in what they want to relate to us about their life, needs and emotions. Unfortunately, in most of our day-to-day conversations, we often do nothing more than pass judgement on what people say: *"That's good." "That's rubbish!" "All you've got to do is this or that." "Well, I think that..."* and so on. Active listening is listening without any form of judgement and getting involved through using questions and reiterations.

Think about this: If you want to know someone properly, you need to realise that talking is not the most essential thing; whereas listening *is*.

ACTION! Talk by all means, but take breaks and leave spaces for the other person to speak. While you are listening, for example, go for reformulations with expressions such as, *"In your opinion..." "You mean to say that..." "You say you feel that when you talk about..." "Deep down, you'd like..."* This makes the person to whom you are talking feel that they are being listened to and helps them open up more easily.

3rd Practical Solution: **Constantly ask yourself, "What is this person really like?"**

A little trick which helps you take a genuine interest in people is to ask yourself inwardly throughout the discussion, *"What is this person standing in front of me really like?"*

If not knowing what to say happens to be what you are afraid of, then let your own curiosity about that person be your guide and questions will come to you naturally. Counter fear with inquisitiveness, which is, by contrast, an enjoyable feeling. It draws you out of your inward ruminations so that you can, quite simply, connect with the other person better.

ACTION! During a meeting, imagine a large question mark over the head of the person to whom you are speaking and ask yourself inwardly what they are really like. Get to know them genuinely by asking them occasional questions. Broadly, there are five themes which can help you get to know a person properly: 1) Their job; 2) Their interests and aspirations; 3) Their weekend leisure activities; 4) Their personality and qualities; 5) Their personal story and relationship with others.

4th Practical Solution: **When you are speaking to someone, use their first name regularly.**

There is one thing we do not think about enough when we talk to other people, be they colleagues or friends, and that is to use their first name. We all have a tendency to chat away and never use the first name of the people we are talking to unless it is to call them, get their attention or give them an order. This includes when we meet people for the first time – we just do not give it any thought. Yet, saying the other person's first name is an expression of interest in them; a mark of attention, because the first name is a person's primary element of identity.

Think about this: When a person calls you often by your first name in a conversation, that means they are interested in you. Have you ever noticed this, or perhaps you do not like it when someone does it? You will particularly remember the person who was most attentive to your first name, especially in a first meeting amongst a group of people.

ACTION! During a discussion, remember from time to time to accompany your questions by the first name of the other person (*First Name + Question*) or when you tell anecdotes (*First Name + Sentences*).

5th Practical Solution: **Discover what topics the other person finds pleasant; their favourite things.**

This is the very best way to get involved in more personal, friendly conversations. Every person has conversational topics that thrill them and which they love talking about for hours on end. If you can pinpoint these and you know how to listen, then you will create a deep connection with that person.

One should definitely bear in mind that most people are frustrated at not being able to talk about subjects which matter to them. They 'censure' themselves in the public sphere and would be only too happy to share their thoughts if you make the effort to understand them.

ACTION! It is hard to guess what these topics might be, so the best thing is to ask the person subtly. Examples: *"What do you like talking about most?" "What things in life thrill you?" "What topics could you talk about all night long?"*

Er, I'm stuck... I'm afraid of being intrusive!

Some people get stuck when they take an interest in other people because they are afraid of ruffling their feathers or seeming intrusive by asking personal questions. This is a mistaken, limiting belief because, often, people are only too happy when others take an interest in them. They gladly answer personal questions if they are asked with tact and in a rational context. As long as you do not fire off a non-stop series of questions like a journalist, there should be no problem!

Remind yourself of the following to help you get round mental blocks with other people:

- Every individual has their ego and there is nothing which pleases them more than the fact that someone is interested in them and that they can share with them whatever is on their mind.

- If you never dare ask any personal questions, then you will only ever know what the other person shows outwardly. This does not help deepen the relationship.

- People do not really pay attention to questions which are too direct (*"And you, are you single?"*) and will usually only reply out of 'social instinct' without wondering why you have asked them.

- At best, the person will answer you and you will gain by getting to know them better. At worst, they will be uncomfortable and not answer. However, they might also answer over the course of the discussion, as they start to feel more at ease.

- Most of the time, people only answer questions about their work or what they have done at the weekend. They would be delighted to answer more personal questions about such things as their hobby, dream, or concern.

INFO SHEET 7

HOW TO PAY A SINCERE COMPLIMENT

Expressing a positive feeling towards another person is an integral part of social communication. It is a factor in strengthening a relationship between two people.

Every human being is attracted to the idea of receiving kind words; a sincere compliment. On the one hand, it is nice and always satisfying for one's self-esteem. On the other hand, it proves that the person to whom you are talking is interested in you and they are letting you know this by mentioning a personal attribute which they appreciate in you.

From a biological point of view, it is an indirect verbal way for an individual to enter your inner sanctum and leave you with a positive token of appreciation. That is why compliments are useful and serve as social glue in forming a bond.

Many people are uncomfortable at the thought of paying a compliment because they feel as if they are being untruthful, manipulative or playing a role... However, this is about paying a *sincere* compliment! Quite obviously, it is best to refrain if our compliment is fake or if we do not have a compliment to pay somebody.

However, the reality is quite different. It turns out that there are many people we appreciate in our circle or amongst those whom we meet. Unfortunately, we never think of letting them know this because we dare not pay a compliment for modesty's sake; or we do not do it because of an ego issue. Yet, deep down, we think that this person has a good heart, that they are wearing a nice shirt, or that they quite simply have brightened up our day...

If I gravitate towards one person rather than another; or if I always hang out with the same friends; if I've been going to the same hairdresser for years; or if I prefer to confide in such and such a psychologist, then there is indeed a reason why, and attributes of theirs which I appreciate – but there you go, I do not necessarily think about paying people compliments.

However, paying a sincere compliment only takes a minute and can win you that person's respect for years.

Finding a compliment to pay should be easy inasmuch as everyday life provides us with a plethora of opportunities:

The compliment might be about the following:	Examples
1) Appearance (physique, style of dress, etc.)	*"That blue dress suits you wonderfully and makes you even more beautiful."*
2) Personality (attitude, character, a personal attribute, etc.)	*"I do love your sensitivity. You have a delightful personality and I always enjoy having these discussions with you."*
3) Something the other person has done, a talent	*"You are very gifted at writing. Tell me, how long have you been a writer?"*
4) The effort that a person goes to for you or puts into a particular activity	*"It's nice working with you because you're always so patient. Thanks for taking the time to explain everything to me."*

Another tip!

Ask yourself the following question: **What is it about other people which creates a positive feeling in me?**

The table above serves as a guide to give you ideas about compliments. However, typically, if you just settle for being sincere and following your heart, then you will have no difficulty in finding something to say. The main thing is that you personalise the compliment.

Practical example:

Genuine feelings	Externalisation through words	The real result:
I think that Mark is a generous person. He's always there to listen to me and help me...	===============> Follow your heart, your instincts	*"Mark, I should tell you that I like you a lot. You're a very generous sort of a person and you're always there for me."*

If you pay untruthful compliments you do not believe in, people might catch on because your words will sound hollow. It goes without saying that paying a person a compliment should take place in an appropriate context (doing it in front of a group of people should be avoided if this could make a person uncomfortable) and it needs to be subtly gauged (repetitions should be avoided).

If you fear that your compliment may seem too out-front or intrusive, you can always compliment someone in the third person.

For example: *"By the way, did you know that Julian told me you were the funniest and most liked person in the group?"*

Or, pay compliments based on facts and not on personal attributes.

For example: *"Thank you for your report. I liked the quality of the work and the fact that it was given in quickly."*

Er, I do want to pay a compliment but I get stuck!

Despite everything, some people get stuck when paying a person a compliment. The reasons may be manifold, and are often of a psychological nature: shyness, modesty, blushing, fear of rejection, ego issues, etc.

Some people confide that they get extremely embarrassed when they have to pay a compliment because it is not something they are used to doing and they just cannot do it openly with people. They pull out heaps of excuses about how they freeze up, and so on... that is, until they are asked the following question as a sort of Eureka moment:

"But what's stopping you from paying the compliment in a text or e-mail to the person you like? It only takes a minute."

There are no more excuses – if you freeze up when you are with the person face to face, then you also have the option of expressing yourself in a text or e-mail and the person will enjoy reading your warm message just as much.

Paying a sincere compliment is a fantastic sign of sociability towards other people and makes your human interactions warmer. So, it would be a pity to miss the opportunity.

PRACTICAL APPLICATION: Find a sincere compliment which you can pay to four people in your circle or whom you come across on a daily basis. List these people and just have a go! You will be pleasantly surprised by their reaction – effect guaranteed!

INFO SHEET 8

KNOWING HOW TO BE CONCILIATORY – WHILST BEING ASSERTIVE!

Having a conciliatory approach with people is a sociability signal vital for maintaining the thread of a successful encounter with others.

It merely consists of going in the same direction as the person with whom you are speaking in order to show them that you are genuinely listening to them and you understand their point of view. It serves to keep a harmonious connection during the interaction.

In reality, a conciliatory attitude is shown by the following few actions:

- ✓ *Genuinely listening*
- ✓ *Simply agreeing: "Yes…" "Ok…" "All right…" "Uh-huh…" "Of course…"*
- ✓ *Nodding your head*
- ✓ *Smiling*
- ✓ *Reformulating their words; paraphrasing what they say*

These behaviour patterns are reassuring for the person to whom you are talking and help them feel at ease with you. Nodding your head and paraphrasing show the person that you are actively seeking to interact with them. Sociable people generally know how to look conciliatory and diplomatic. The opposite of a conciliatory attitude would be a systematic adversarial approach which would cut short any social interaction!

In regard to reformulation, you have two options during the discussion:
- either highlight the other person's last words, or
- highlight a piece of information you like.
For example: *"When you say you went to see a play, do you mean…"*

Nevertheless, knowing how to be conciliatory does not mean that you are going to concur with everything the other person says to you. The idea is not to say 'yes' and nod your head all the time! Quite the reverse, too much of a conciliatory attitude can be counter-productive and expose the deepest kind of inner problems within a person, such as poor self-esteem, shyness, fear of rejection, lack of personality, and so on.

Looking conciliatory = a sociability signal

HOWEVER, MAKE SURE YOU DIFFERENTIATE BETWEEN:

Appearing conciliatory without being assertive = a too nice, reticent attitude; someone who lets things happen

Appearing conciliatory whilst being assertive = a healthy attitude which is true to oneself

Self-affirmation is a necessity for every individual: it is about accepting what one wants to say deep down. In other words, it is about being true to one's profound desires, thoughts and values.

If you always show yourself to be conciliatory with the person to whom you are speaking but deep down you do not approve of anything he or she does or says (examples: constantly being late for work; loud, aggressive tone of voice; political opinions, etc.), and this happens every day as a matter of course, then your attitude will quite simply be incongruous.

In the same way, when we do not like a situation, we tend to keep quiet for fear of annoying people and to avoid making matters worse. However, this attitude can create frustration and hostility towards the people concerned. Sooner or later, things will flare up if you do not communicate with other people sufficiently and keep everything pent up.

You absolutely do have the option of appearing conciliatory whilst asserting yourself! In the following chart, we shall go through **a variety of self-affirmation techniques** which can provide you with practical solutions.

S T A T I N G A N E E D	• The formula created by <u>Thomas Gordon</u>: **"When you…"** (state facts without interpretation) **…I feel…** (express the emotion or feeling) **…because I need…** (express one's own need) **…so, I'm asking you…** (seek redress) **…to…"** (express an incentive for the other person) • Avoid "**YOU + criticism**" (= judgement) and go for "**I + my feeling**" • Know how to say 'no' if required: Instead of "**I can't**", say "**I don't want to.**"	<u>Example expressed with judgement/criticism:</u> "It's your fault I'm bored! You never want to go out! You're always at your computer and busy working! I'm fed up!" <u>Example expressing what is felt, without judgement/criticism:</u> "Alan, when you're always at your computer or busy working, I feel a bit sad and lonely. I need to spend more time with you and the kids. I know you've got a lot of work on at the moment but I'd really like you to make an effort for us. We're a family and we need you."
A S K I N G	Find **the right words** to make a request: I'd like… + my feelings I want you to… + my feelings I'd appreciate it if you... + my feelings *"I don't suppose you'd do me a favour and...?"* *"Can I rely on you to...?"* *"Sorry to bother you but...?"*	<u>Example of a request formulated as an order:</u> *"You really get on my nerves with your football! Can't you switch to another channel?"* <u>Example of a tactfully formulated request:</u> *"I'm getting a bit bored with this. You know, football isn't really my cup of tea. I don't suppose you'd do me a favour and switch to another channel so we can watch something*

		we're both interested in?"
C R I T I C I S I N G	>> Never criticise personality, but instead **a behavioural trait**; a measurable action. >> Instead of criticising the person directly, highlight **the unpleasant consequences** to you or the group. >> Precede a criticism with **a kind word or compliment** to create a positive atmosphere. >> End the criticism on **a positive note**: *"I know I can rely on you."* >> Simply ask **a question** to understand the person's viewpoint: *"Why do you think that...?"* *"You don't think that...?"*	Example of insensitive criticism: *"You're too fastidious! You must have vacuumed the area behind me ten times over! You're really annoying me!* Example of appropriate criticism: *"You know I've always admired your sense of tidiness but don't you think that vacuuming once is enough? I don't know whether you've noticed but you've gone over the same place several times in the last ten minutes..."* Example of appropriate criticism: *"Watch out, because every time you arrive late, you oblige the entire group to wait for you and our customers will get fed up. You really must make sure you come to work twenty minutes earlier."*

INFO SHEET 9

KNOWING HOW TO USE HUMOUR
TO CONNECT WITH SOMEONE

Using humour and levity is the most effective way to get closer to other people and defuse awkward situations. Making people laugh creates a feeling of well-being in them and quickly establishes a close connection. This explains why humour remains a formidable mechanism to expedite the forming of relationships.

Nevertheless, if laughing does not come easily to you and you are a rather serious type, there is no point in forcing yourself! A sense of humour is not absolutely required. Remember that you have an arsenal of ten different sociability signals available to you to present yourself as being sociable and popular with other people.

Having a slight sense of humour or taking things light-heartedly is essential. It is quite enough to enable you to fit in with others.

If you study the most sociable types of people carefully, they do not necessarily tell many jokes or laugh all the time but they do smile a lot and know how to take things in a cheerful spirit.

In this info sheet, we shall list a number of ways to assist those who want to develop their sense of humour.

The purpose is to demonstrate that humour is of use and can help you in your social interactions:

- Laughing and smiling are universal characteristics shared by all human beings whatever their fields of interest.[22]
- It follows on that every individual is susceptible to humour and that there are things which make them laugh which you can use to get closer to them.
- Showing a sense of humour has a potent two-fold effect: it not only helps you feel good and provides you with release, but also produces a feeling of happiness in the other person.
- Humour is catching, creating a good atmosphere within a group and quickly getting rid of any awkward moments or periods of silence.

As such, whether or not you have a sense of humour, it would be a shame to be without it. With it, you will make your life and that of others that bit more pleasant. Deep down, you have comic potential because you have a mouth with which to laugh and smile! The first thing to do to make this work is to pluck up the courage and want to make other people laugh. As follows below, we are going to look at some ideas to help you develop your sense of humour.

---

4 TIPS TO REMEMBER

● **Pinpoint what makes you smile or laugh:**
There must be topics or situations which readily elicit laughter from you.
This is the most natural way to help you use humour with other people without having to force yourself. So, the idea is to pinpoint these subjects and then introduce them into your conversations.
Examples: talk about a film you find funny; your favourite comedian; hilarious situations which arose on a trip, and so on.

● **Pinpoint what makes the other person smile or laugh:**
In the same way, you can find out what things other people find funny. You will find this to be a timesaver and it will help you form a close tie with them.
The best solution is to ask them because you cannot guess: *"What makes you laugh the most?" "What things in life do you find funny?"*

● **Go for self-deprecation:**
If you tend to be a rather socially awkward person, or have very noticeable shortcomings, accept them instead of hiding them – exploit them. This is THE best way to be at ease with others whilst being different.
Indeed, there are people who come to terms with having their head in the clouds and being anxious and reclusive. They cheerfully make the best of it when they talk about it. This is a radical solution to laugh off their uneasiness and overcome the fear of how other people perceive them.

● **Draw inspiration from people who make you laugh:**
Watch TV sitcoms (Friends, The Big Bang Theory) and your favourite stand-up comedians, (George Carlin, Eddie Murphy) and take notes. Draw inspiration from their attitude and puns. Observing

---

others can help you develop your own sense of humour and bring your real self to light. It is vital you do not miss out on this since it gives you ideas!

Valuable resources:

https://www.wikihow.com/develop-a-sense-of-humor: Illustrated article with ideas to develop your sense of humour.
https://news.yahoo.com/odd: A website to give you ideas for weird or funny anecdotes to share with people.
https://www.rd.com/jokes: A website to give you plenty of jokes to tell, categorised by theme.

INFO SHEET 10

SHOWING YOUR APPRECIATION TO OTHERS, EXPRESSING YOUR GRATITUDE

Neuroscience proves that the practice of gratitude increases the feeling of happiness and has a highly beneficial effect on health. This includes a reduction of stress hormones, an increase in the level of oxytocin, and a better quality of sleep.[23] *(Studies by Dr. Emmons & Dr. McCullough, 2003.)*

Showing our appreciation to someone means that we articulate our friendly feelings, conveying the message that we appreciate them and the fact that they are there for us.

Every human being needs to receive tokens of gratitude and affection. This pertains not only to couples but also to our family, friends and colleagues.

Although we might spend a lot of time with our friends, they are not necessarily aware of how much we value them. Most of them do not even know that we consider them to be friends, which is a sad reality. Give that some thought!

Many people are friends with each other but few express their appreciation or their feelings to their friend or relation. This is a shame because it would help strengthen the bond and nurture a genuine, friendly relationship.

In practical terms, showing one's appreciation to someone else can take the form of considerate words, such as the following:
"I appreciate you a lot." "Thank you for being here." "You mean a lot to me." "I value our friendship." "Don't forget that if you have a problem you can call me," and so on.

For some of you, these phrases might appear hackneyed or laughable in a friendly relationship. It would be a mistake to think like this because human beings do not only have romantic feelings but friendly sentiments too.

It does not occur to us often enough to articulate these things and show sincerity to people we like. If a friend said these nice, cordial words to you during a conversation, frankly, what effect would that have on you?

At that very moment, you would be touched and **know how much that person values you** and that they consider you to be a friend.

Often, a true friendship begins with this mutual exchange of sincere words. These thoughtful tokens show that you appreciate that person. Words are free; they do not cost you anything and, most importantly, they make other people feel good. So, why not do it?

Additionally, the more you show signs of thoughtfulness to others, the more you will receive in return. However, do not do it with the aim of gaining something. They must be sincere and spontaneous!

Expressing your appreciation to others is vital in a friendly relationship, helping to strengthen the bond considerably.

If you are a bashful person or clamming up prevents you from doing this, the following reasons might convince you to get over that hurdle:

• Expressing your appreciation to another person often only consists of uttering a single sentence which actually takes you just a few seconds!

• You will never lose out because your friend will be touched and cherish your gesture. Even if he or she appears to be demure or silent, they will not forget it and will know how much you value them.

• Do not take it personally if your friend does not return the term of endearment because it might be something they find hard to do at that particular time. However, he or she may well get round to doing it one day; on your birthday, for instance. Everyone is free to decide for themselves whether they accept or reject a gesture of affection.

• If you are afraid of feeling uncomfortable or making the other person uneasy when face to face, remember that you still have the option of saying it in an e-mail or text – so, there is no longer any excuse!

• People always prefer an awkwardly expressed gesture of thoughtfulness to nothing at all!

It would be a shame to think that only love is entitled to the exchange of considerate tokens when such a thing can exist between friends and family too! Upbringing and society do not encourage us to express our feelings to others.

Some people feel very uncomfortable with ready-made sentences and phrases, but practical examples are definitely necessary to help the shyest people or those who have no idea what to say. With practice, this will become natural.

SOME IDEAS FOR SHOWING YOUR APPRECIATION TO OTHERS:

Show your friends affection by calling them little names
Examples: *"My Nico," "My dear," "My pal," "Gorgeous,"* etc.

Express sincere feelings about your conversations
Examples: *"I miss our discussions," "It's great to talk with you," "We have fun, don't we!"* etc.

Show the other person that they are important to you
Examples: *"You're my best friend," "You can rely on me," "I'm here if you need me," "It's a good thing you're around!"* etc.

Use friendly little gestures
- Placing a tender, companionable hand on the shoulder of a sad friend can warm their heart.
- Give a close friend a big affectionate hug before they go to live in a new town.

Show your gratitude; give wholehearted thanks
This is about recognising someone's true worth. The thought of saying 'thank you' to our friends does not occur to us often enough. Most people never even say it once. If we search deep down, there are plenty of times in our lives when there is cause to thank a friend for being there, for their considerate gestures or a service rendered. Remind them of that particular moment and thank them verbally; or with a personalised gift; or a handwritten letter.

Pay a compliment; use flattering expressions (reread Info Sheet 6)
Robert Orben used to say, *"A compliment is verbal sunshine."*

Everybody has their own preferred tokens of attention – some people feel uncomfortable with compliments or physical contact whereas others will be highly receptive. It is up to you to sense what might please your friends and family, depending on their attitude.

PRACTICAL APPLICATION: If you are finding it hard to swing into action, set yourself challenges by taking three ideas from the list below and trying to use them on your friends over the course of the week. Observe their reaction.

You should not view this as carrying out cold, calculating exercises but as a human means **to improving your social relationships and reinvigorating them**.

 Ask yourself these questions frankly...
They should persuade you to take action!

• When was the last time you said 'thank you' to a friend?

• When was the last time you told someone how important they are to you?

• When was the last time you gave a friend a warm hug?

• Have you already received such gestures of amity from a friend; and did you really reciprocate?

INFO SHEET 11

KNOWING HOW TO TAKE THE INITIATIVE SO AS NOT TO REMAIN PASSIVE

Sometimes when you go out, it may happen that people rebuke you for being too passive and quiet. They get especially irritated by pregnant pauses in conversation with you. This can be understood from a human point of view – your friends like to have enthusiastic people to talk to and who seek to interact with them on a frequent basis.

When in a large group (4 to 10 people), you can simply go for available social communication (ASC), because there will always be people who take it upon themselves to keep conversations going. However, in a small group or a one-to-one situation (2 to 3 people), it goes without saying that the ASC method will prove insufficient; you will have to take practical steps to assert your presence!

In such a case, the person to whom you are talking might get bored and be left with a bad feeling about the meeting. So, it is vital that you help him or her to feel more at ease by showing initiative.

Below is our suggested list of ideas so that you do not remain passive.

LIST OF PRACTICAL INITIATIVES

What matters is encouraging interaction between a person and you: That is ten times more important than the substance of what you say!

<u>During a simple chat</u>, when you feel a deafening silence setting in...

1) *Get the person to talk by asking open-ended questions*

   Example: *"I like the atmosphere in this place. What do you think of it?"*

2) *Tell an interesting or funny anecdote*

   Example: *"Incidentally, guess what happened to me this week as I was getting on the tube. I..."*

---

3) *Talk about yourself*

   Example: *"Last Saturday, I went hiking in the forest, and then on Sunday I watched TV. I remember that..."*

4) *Suggest an activity*

   Example: *"Hey, let's go for a walk along the bank of the Thames — or maybe you'd like to go somewhere else?"*

If you want to keep a relationship going when it comes to a hiatus...

5) *Send a message to the person to find out how they are.*

   Example: *"So, how was your stay in the mountains? Are you feeling better?"*

6) *Give some of your own news*

   Example: *"I passed the entrance exam to my Teacher's Training Course. I'm so pleased about that!"*

7) *Proffer an invitation*

   Example: *"By the way, there's an All-Night Festival this weekend. Do you fancy going?"*

INFO SHEET 12

LEARNING HOW TO APPROACH OTHERS

Approaching a person on their own territory is **a sign of your availability**. You show yourself to be 'on the scene' and you give them the opportunity of interacting with you.

Amongst all the signs of availability, the aforementioned is the most important one because, without fail, you initiate a human interaction straightaway. However, some people dare not approach others out of shyness or their lack of confidence. Others do not do it because they are not in the mood or feeling well on that particular day. As a result, they isolate themselves in a corner, when, deep down, in reality they hope to have social contact just like everyone else.

Bear in mind that the only thing which counts is the act of approaching another person, since you can break off interaction at any time with or without justification, but simply in a courteous manner; such as, smiling as you part. It tends to happen like that everywhere, at parties or group outings, where blunders and embarrassment can occur frequently! Natural affinity will decide how the interaction progresses. If people see that you are no longer sending out signs of availability, they will realise subconsciously, and end up moving away of their own accord to find someone else to talk to. So, no need to panic – just assume your role.

This info sheet does not aim to present a 'magic formula' ensuring that you find it in your nature to approach others. However, it does provide some tips to help you make that first step in approaching others.

<u>Here is a list of positive thoughts</u>
<u>to tell yourself the day before you go out or when you go out</u>

Repeat them like a mantra to spur you on!

Thought No. 1: *"If I approach others, I'll give myself the opportunity of making a new, meaningful encounter."*

Thought No. 2: *"Something very nice happened to me the last*

---

time I approached other people: [...]" (Write down this positive recollection.)

Thought No. 3: *"I'll certainly be safe if I stay in my corner but I'll remain by myself. If I force myself to approach others, I might make a new friend."*

Thought No. 4: *"I first became acquainted with the people I liked most in my life, [...], because of the effort I made to open up to them. I'll do the same thing again when I go out this time."* (Write down their first names within the square brackets.)

Thought No. 5: *"The hardest part will be the first 15-30 seconds. All it takes to assume my role is a 15-30 second effort – I'll show myself to be available to others."*

Thought No. 6: *"Other people are not there to judge me. Deep down, they're also expecting me to make the first move because everybody wants to forge ties."*

INFO SHEET 13

KNOWING WHAT TO SAY IN THOSE FIRST FEW MINUTES OF INTERACTION

When people go out or attend a party, many freeze up at the thought of approaching a stranger because they often do not know what to say in those first few minutes of interaction. Indeed, it is hardly easy given that they have never spoken with that person and have to strike up a cordial conversation as if they knew each other. The difficulty of this exercise varies depending on the context and it is advisable to personalise your approach according to the context of the event. For the shyest amongst you, we provide you with examples of dialogue below to give you some ideas to help you take the plunge!

Context: *"In a private area"* such as an evening out, a social event, or party, etc.	Context: *"In a public area"* such as at a library, in public transport, in a park, etc.
You *"Hi!"*	**You** *"Hello"*
The other person *"Hi!"*	**The other person** *"Hello"*
You *"My name's Oliver. What's yours?"*	**You** *"Excuse me. I happened to see you're holding a brochure about cultural and sports activities in Windsor. I was wondering what sort of interesting activities they've got going on because I live in Windsor too..."*
The other person *"Kate."*	
You *"Is this the first time you've been here?"*	**The other person** *"Er, oh, right? They've got open air cinema, and there're also introductory yoga and meditation classes."*
The other person *"Yes, it's the first time I've come to this event."*	
You *"Ah, yes. By the way, what's your line of work? I'm studying*	**You** *"Ah, that's of interest to me because I've been looking for that sort of recreational activity. I think they're*

filmmaking."

The other person
"I'm a student at a business school"

You
"Which school is that? Because I've got friends who are also at business school. They tell me the first years are the hardest!"

The other person
"Oh, really? I'm at LBS. I'm doing a degree and I can confirm that!"

You
"But, hey! I'm not going to bore you talking about your studies! Do you have hobbies? What do you usually like to do at the weekend?"

not easy to find and I'm the kind of person to miss out on all my own town's activities! ;-)"

The other person
"You can find out all about it at the town hall or library. Besides, with the Internet, it's really easy to find free activities in your town."

You
"And what about you – do you do meditation or yoga?"

The other person
"Yes. In fact, I only started three months ago! ;-) I was looking for a relaxing activity I could do in a group. I find that more inspiring."

You
"By the way, what's your name? I'm Anthony..."

Sometimes, we can become anxious when we conduct an initial conversation. Anyone would think it was incredibly tricky to find words but the first few minutes of most discussions resemble the two examples given above. That is how it goes at the majority of social events and meetings! Fairly simple, light-hearted words lead to more meaningful discussion later on.

Simply remember the following in your social interactions:

- Most of the time, the first discussions start with a trivial sentence.
  Examples: *"It's really dreadful weather today." "What's your first name?" "This is the first time I've come here. Do you know...?"*

- The act of making contact with people differs according to location. It is good to personalise your approach depending on the context. Raise a subject associated with the place, the theme of the event, or a distinctive feature of the person to whom you are talking, so that they know why you are approaching them.

Examples: *"Do you like this kind of music?" "Is the food good?" "Hey, you're wearing a Manchester United t-shirt..."* etc.

- It is important to give yourself a brief introduction (say your first name and what you do). This brings you out of anonymity and quickly reassures the other person.

- If you want to create a connection and get into a more personal discussion, you absolutely must direct the conversation towards the other person's interests and hobbies. You can begin by asking them what their job is and then move on to their interests...

SUMMARY:

**The first few minutes of
a successful conversation**

1) Greeting phase

2) Suggest the reason why you are approaching
   them (depending on the context)

3) Introduction phase

4) Direct the conversation towards interests
   and hobbies

INFO SHEET 14

KNOWING WHAT TO SAY TO CLOSE AN INTERACTION

This final stage is what is called the separation phase. Some people do not know what to say or are embarrassed when it comes to conducting those last few minutes of an interaction when people say goodbye to each other. There can be multiple reasons for this: bashfulness; fear of upsetting the other person by interrupting them; concern at attracting the attention of the group to oneself if one wants to leave before the others, and so on.

Most people are afraid of not knowing what to say when what matters most is knowing how to keep it simple and courteous. Here are a few examples of separation phrases:

"Excuse me, but I have to go. I'll be seeing you."
"I'm afraid I'll have to leave you now. See you around."

If you are afraid of upsetting the person to whom you are talking, you also have the following four options:

• Give a reason as to why you are leaving	*"I have to go because my wife's at home waiting for me."*
• Pay a sincere compliment before leaving:	*"Well, it's been a pleasure. I really enjoyed talking to you about..."*
• Say goodbye, smiling, or using a warm or affectionate gesture	*"Let me give you a big hug, Laura. I do have to go now."*
• Suggest that you are going to meet again in any case:	*"Right, we'll see each other in a week, then. Have a safe trip home and a lovely evening."* •

If these are work colleagues who you see regularly at the office, you can use the last example above, suggesting that you will be seeing each other soon: *"Well, Simon, I'll see you tomorrow, then..."*

In any case, your colleagues can feel instinctively from your body language that you are on the verge of leaving. They know your discreet character, are used to your low-profile image and the fact that you do not like to linger at the office. They will not hold it against you as long as you remain courteous. It is far better to say goodbye to people whilst smiling amicably than to ignore them every time you leave.

The problem may be that you fear attracting the group's attention if you leave first. However, if you do not heed your initial desire to leave, then you risk putting up with interminable discussion, a long wait and in the long run, being the last person to leave!

Observe how people say goodbye to you on a daily basis. It is pretty quick most of the time – a few brief words and a friendly gesture right in the middle of a telephone call or conversation with a customer. That is why you really do not need to get in a state about these things. If you have to go, do it by taking your leave of each person. In the end, what matters is being straightforward and courteous.

How to close an interaction if it is a first meeting

If it is a social situation where you are meeting people for the first time during a group outing, and you do not know how to bring an interaction to a close, there are two scenarios:

• **If you do not take to the other person,** use the previous examples to say goodbye to them or simply give them a parting smile and wave, as most people do at a party when they are looking to interact immediately with someone else in the group. Obviously, the way you do this depends on the context of leaving. Moreover, in any event, if people see that you are no longer sending them any signs of availability, they move off of their own accord anyway!

Nothing is stopping you from coming to terms with what you want and voicing it courteously: *"Well, lovely to have met you. I'm going to mingle with the others a bit now. I'll see you later..."*

• **If you have a genuine affinity for the person you are talking to** but have to bring the interaction to a close, remember in this instance to take care over the way you part if you want to forge ties with this person later on.

One often thinks that the separation phase merely consists of saying goodbye correctly to the other person but if you have no physical means of staying in contact with them, you are not likely to see them again! How many people have you met at some point in your life and regretted not having asked them for an e-mail address or phone number!

Remember this: *Friendship does not start when you say 'hello' but when you say 'goodbye'!*

In this scenario, the manner in which you close the interaction is of great importance. To find a way to see them again, you need to know more about the person. There are four solutions:

1) Ask upfront for their phone number:	*"By the way, do you have a phone number so we can keep in touch?"*
2) Suggest an activity which might interest them so that you can see them again:	*"By the way, there's a Manga exhibition in Paris next month – would you fancy going?"*
3) Invite them directly:	*"I'm throwing a party for my friends at my place this Saturday. Would you like to come..."*
4) Ask for their Facebook:	*"Are you on Facebook? I like using it to stay in touch with people."*

If you do not ask the person these things before leaving, then you can assume that you will never see that person again. This advice might seem obvious to you but it does not necessarily occur to everyone! Sometimes, we seek to bring an interaction to a quick close without realising the significance our last exchange of words can have and how they can decide the future.

INFO SHEET 15

'CONNECT-QUESTIONS': THOSE MAGIC QUESTIONS WHICH CREATE CONNECTIONS

"How are you?" is the most asked question in the world. Yet, people are for the most part in social representation mode between each other and appear to be asking this question without sincerely caring about how people are REALLY.

The reasons explaining this general trend can be mere social reflex, politeness, fear of being intrusive, passivity, and so on.

Be it at work or in our circle of friends or family, there are questions which can make all the difference and create connections between people.

When you are with your friends, instead of holding forth or speaking about various topics for hours on end, bear in mind that a simple question can give quite a different orientation to your conversation, making it more genuine and human.

There are 'magic questions' which make it possible to learn more about a person in a few minutes than you would in several years.

EXAMPLES OF 'CONNECT-QUESTIONS'

It only takes you 2 SECONDS to say!

- How's the world treating you?
- What have you been thinking about most these past few days?
- What do you need?
- Are you coping?
- Are you in good health?
- What can I do for you?
- What would please you?
- What can I do to help you?
- Do you need anything?

If you do not ask people these things, you will only ever see the superficial side that people want to show you, i.e., a social image, a façade.

Daring to do this has a number of advantages and enables you to:

- Get out of shallow conversations and progress towards a more personal tone;
- Get to know people and their needs properly;
- Create a stronger, more genuine bond.

At work, although hierarchical relations exist between individuals, there is nothing preventing a boss from appearing human and attentive for a few minutes with an employee to find out how they are really doing in their job. It is always nice to feel one is being listened to and cared about and that employee will then be more likely to come to work with enthusiasm and a smile on their face.

In the same way, in any of our relationships it can happen that things may not be going well for a friend and we feel powerless to help out during the difficult times they may be going through. As we cannot guess what they expect of us, the best approach is to ask them the question: *"What could I do to help you out or to please you?"* This type of question allows the problem to be resolved in two seconds, and means you will not remain a spectator to their distress.

'Connect-questions' are 'magical' because they can breathe new life into an interaction which otherwise was doomed to failure or stagnation, and can be used to reinvigorate the bonds between people.

INFO SHEET 16

KNOWING HOW TO PLEASE SOMEONE
OR HELP A FRIEND

The topic covered by this info sheet might overlap with some of the themes previously mentioned, such as 'expressing one's gratitude' or 'paying sincere compliments'. However, it aims to complement those info sheets further and suggest other innovative solutions.

A very effective way of building and strengthening a friendly relationship is to know how to please people we like. This does not necessarily occur to us because often we are too focused on ourselves and our own ego. However, knowing how to please others helps us GET CLOSER to them.

As we shall see, there are a variety of ways to please other people, such as compliments, tokens of thoughtfulness, personalised little gifts, and so forth. In short, these are simple things which anyone can do.

Every human on Earth has needs and secret desires whose fulfilment would please him or her straightaway and help them be happier in life. Whether it is your brother, mother or best friend, there are things, small thoughtful gestures, which can gratify them quickly and bring a smile to their faces.

We all have needs, problems to solve and concerns. Knowing people's needs and finding shared concerns makes it possible to get closer to them and develop genuine relationships.

Knowing how to please people is the best way to reach them and make them feel that they are important to you. As a result, it is a real catalyst for strengthening a bond.

If a friend of yours were to remember your birthday or be sincerely interested in your projects, or he or she offered to help you, would that not touch you? Would you not want that person to be your friend?

In human relationships, small thoughtful gestures towards others make all the difference. At each one of your encounters, remember to pinpoint people's personal needs, even if you have to ask them what they are. It is an excellent excuse to connect with them and maintain contact.

GETTING TO KNOW HOW TO PLEASE OTHERS
WITH SMALL ACTIONS

• Ask people upfront what would please them

This is the best solution for finding out people's needs and avoiding speculation. You cannot guess, so you might as well ask tactfully.

Examples: *"What do you like best in life?" "What do you need?" "What could bring a smile to your face in two seconds?"*

• Wish your friends "Happy Birthday!"

A birthday is a symbolic day which is of great importance to lots of people. Remembering this date and wishing someone happy birthday is a strong signal that you care. So, always remember to note down the dates of your friends' birthdays and send them a message on the big day!

• Give personalised little gifts

People love being given presents. Caution – we are not talking about big gifts which cost you a lot of money, and still less do we mean predictable presents, such as boxes of chocolates. What we are talking about here are unique, personalised gifts, i.e., those which are intended solely for that person. Accordingly, you have to have taken a genuine interest in the person to find out what they like.

Examples: a nice handwritten letter; a personalised greetings card; a free ticket to a yoga class; a book or film which they might enjoy, et cetera.

• Dedicate a day to them; spend some real time with them.

Put away your mobile telephone and forget your job. Spend some quality time with your friend and give them your undivided attention. Your heartfelt presence is the most wonderful gift you can give someone.

Examples: go for a walk with them; listen to their troubles and reassure them; watch a film or do cooking together, and so on.

• Make yourself useful; help out

Ask them upfront how you can help out or do them a favour. That will touch them. Every person has needs and worries to sort out on a daily basis. Furthermore, altruism makes the brain happier.[24] We cannot help everyone but we can at least help someone!

Examples: help your friend advance his or her projects; go shopping together; or correct the spelling in the letter accompanying their job application, etc.

● **Surprise him or her**
People always enjoy a pleasant surprise. It might be little things which you do not do with your friend usually. Ask yourself what might give him or her a nice surprise – and go ahead and do it! You are sure to think of something!

Every time you feel the relationship is stagnating, or you sense that it is going nowhere, remember this list. It will give you ideas of how to please others and reinvigorate the relationship!

Whoever the person in front of you is, there are always little routines which can help you get closer to them and create a more human connection.

INFO SHEET 17

HOW TO HAVE A GENUINE CONVERSATION

Knowing how to be genuine with others is fundamental if you are to succeed in attracting the right sort of people and building strong ties.

Of course, in day-to-day life, it is impossible to disclose oneself totally because of the influence of social norms. However, in this instance, it is all about learning how to reveal our true nature at meetings with our friends.

If you are only satisfied by talking about work, then you will have a colleague-like relationship. If you only ever talk about trivial things or leisure pursuits, then you will have a comradely relationship, and so on.

If you limit yourself to playing a role and keeping up a masquerade, it will be tricky to create a true, deep, intimate bond.

At some point, **you will have to take risks** and chat about things which you have on your mind (your dreams, moods, secrets, and so on). This is vital if you are to have strong, genuine relationships with people.

Until you do this, you will have to put up with conversations that other people impose on you. Your relationships will remain at the 'niceties level' to which you have chosen to limit them, as decided by your topics of conversation.

Honest discussion can save relationships and avoid either one of the parties concealing their suffering or frustration, which will orientate the interaction towards a worthwhile outcome.

Furthermore, one must bear in mind that most of our encounters in life are transitory and unfortunately we never see these people ever again! That is why it is important to learn how to be genuine so that we can show others who we are and are able to connect with people who mean something to us.

If you conduct yourself in this way, you will also help others to be genuine and bold enough to speak from the heart.

SOME TIPS
TO BRING ABOUT A HEARTFELT CONVERSATION

● **Accepting one's own true personality**

You cannot be genuine with others if you are constantly playing a role. Your personal atypical side and quirks might well scare off some individuals but will nevertheless attract those people who are right for you. This sorts out the 'wheat from the chaff' which is vital if genuine friendships are what you are really seeking.

So, put aside your yearning to fit in with a group, reject any set phrases, such as *"I must..."* and concentrate solely on *"Who I really am..."*

● **Speak plainly from the heart; express your feelings**

Every time we open our mouths, we tend to self-censor our words automatically and adjust ourselves in relation to the other person's attitude. What if we took the chance of putting ourselves in a bit of jeopardy – such as speaking sincerely, with spontaneity and without the least calculation?

Go for such phrases as: *"I feel..." "I'd like..." "I sense..."* and so forth.

● **Establish personal and very specific topics of discussion**

- Your interests and aspirations in life
- Your problems and worries which preoccupy you
- Your secrets and background

Feel free to make a list of three facts about yourself which might help you let go.

● **Encourage the other person to share their emotions**

Rephrase expressions of feelings: *"So, that's what you're sad about..." "So, you'd like..."* etc.

● **Ask the right questions to encourage a genuine conversation**

Use 'connect-questions': *"What do you need?" "How's life treating you?"* and so on.

INFO SHEET 18

HOW TO HAVE GREATER SELF-CONFIDENCE WHEN WITH OTHERS

One often confuses self-confidence with self-esteem but the two terms do not have the same meaning.

Self-esteem is an evaluation a person makes of their own self-worth; and the love they have for themselves.

Self-confidence is the belief a person has in their own ability to succeed or take effective action in a particular field.

When I look at myself in the mirror, I might consider myself to be worthless and dull (= negative self-esteem due to a low opinion of myself). However, at the same time, as I love cooking and playing tennis, both of which I do regularly, I know I can prepare an excellent meal and play a good game (= good self-confidence because of my experience in those fields).

In human relationships, it can be a problem when a person constantly denigrates him or herself inwardly, and thinks of themself as worthless or dull when they come into contact with others.

As a result, the person is inhibited. They dare not speak, and avoid making themselves noticed. In social situations, they are afraid of how they are perceived by others and consequently appear to be unassuming.

This becomes a vicious circle because the person is marked by negative experiences at previous encounters. They are likely to be disheartened when in company, and tend ever more towards avoidance and isolation.

Therefore, to avoid distress, it is important not to let these problems linger. Below, we have compiled a list of potential solutions to help you have more self-confidence and become bold enough to interact with others.

A FEW TIPS TO ACQUIRE MORE
SELF-CONFIDENCE WHEN INTERACTING WITH OTHERS

● Get to know yourself well; make a list of your positive attributes:

No, you are not worthless or dull! You have to learn to respect yourself and not just see your shortcomings. Until you stop being obsessed with your faults, you will fear being judged by others and feel ill-at-ease in your interactions. What you have to say can also be of interest to people.

► Write down three of your qualities in a notebook. Concentrate on these when you are with others.

► Make these into positive affirmations, like little routines to help your brain absorb them. For example: *"People like chatting with me."* Say it to yourself before going to sleep and when you wake up in the morning...

● Note down your accomplishments; the things you have managed to do with others:

If you lack confidence when you meet people, think back to positive experiences you have had and list them in a notebook. When you are feeling anxious, reread this 'list of achievements'. Examples: a meeting which went well; a lively discussion you had; a smile you extracted from somebody...

● Remind yourself that you are fallible – accept and embrace this fact:

Amongst existing solutions, there is one which consists of coming to terms with your inadequacies and avoiding attempts to hide them at all costs (blushing, physical complexes, awkwardness). The more you battle against these faults, the more you will feel uncomfortable when they do crop up. Accept the fact that people you are with might notice them. Accept that you might stumble over your words, etc. Assume your special personality and go for humour and self-deprecation.

● Go for it and take action! Speak up!

The best solution for acquiring more self-confidence remains that of taking action. So, you are afraid of approaching people, talking about yourself, paying a compliment – well, stop hesitating and go for it! Try once; try two, three or four times. It will be extremely awkward to begin with but with experience you will feel more confident and comfortable. Still have doubts? Think back to your positive experiences.

INFO SHEET 19

OVERCOMING YOUR AUTOMATIC NEGATIVE THOUGHTS

This info sheet aims to complement the previous one. There are people who have such limiting thoughts in their heads that they remain focused on their unease throughout an entire meeting, instead of enjoying the present moment.

These automatic negative thoughts can be of the following type: *"I'm worthless" "He's not going to understand me in any case" "I'm not interesting enough" "I'm going to disturb him,"* amongst others.

The problem with these automatic thoughts is that they are, for the most part, irrational and limit you significantly in your human interactions.

For instance, imagine a person who wants to learn how to talk about themselves and introduce themselves to others but who is constantly afraid of being misunderstood or boring people. For as long as they have these intrusive thoughts, they will find it hard to take action, or they will do so in an incredibly awkward way.

To do well, your inner discourse must be changed and automatic thoughts have to be replaced with more suitable, positive thoughts.

Generally speaking, when you experience mental blocks when you are with others, it is because there is a profound reason for this and limiting notions might be the source of your sense of paralysis.

Ask yourself about the nature of these dysfunctional thoughts; identify them carefully; and reform them.

EXAMPLES OF **Automatic negative thoughts**	**Positive, suitable thoughts** What I should tell myself instead:
I'm worthless and dull	=> My positive attributes mean I too have something to offer other people.
I'm going to bore this person	=> People are always inquisitive and want to know more about each other.

This person is going to notice my faults	=> They have better things to do than pay attention to my faults.
There's no point	=> I could always do with a new friend or with learning things.
I feel misunderstood	=> If I truly open up, people will understand me.
This person's already got loads of friends	=> Having loads of friends doesn't mean having *real* friends.

PRACTICAL APPLICATION: Make a two-column table like the one above. On the left, list your dysfunctional thoughts so that you can become aware of your mental blocks and learn how to replace them with more suitable thoughts in the right-hand column.

It is vital you work on yourself because it is these dysfunctional thoughts which are preventing you from interacting or connecting with others. Invariably, you always find some sort of an excuse for yourself subconsciously, but if you change your way of thinking, then there is a strong likelihood that you will make good on subsequent occasions.

Obviously, you are not going to get rid of your limiting beliefs in just a few days. This exercise is something which should be undertaken regularly over time. A good piece of news is that the brain is neuroplastic;[25] that is, it is malleable and can be changed over the course of various experiences. The brain can dispose of old thought patterns and replace them with new ones which will develop into a new habit. So, nothing is set in stone; hence, the importance of acting shrewdly.

SOME MORE TIPS TO OVERCOME YOUR NEGATIVE THOUGHTS

● **Breathe and focus on the present moment:**
Instead of struggling against a tide of thoughts which floods you and often ends up getting the upper hand, let these negative thoughts flow through you and accommodate them as you breathe deeply. Sometimes, it is better to learn how to skirt round something rather than wearing yourself out – surf the waves, so to speak: do not fight against the current but become one with the water...

Breathe in and out, focusing your attention on the here and now – your senses, the sounds, the smells, the beauty of the surroundings and the voice of the person to whom you are talking. Try to feel rather than think!

• Turn fear into pleasure:

If you are afraid of approaching others, try to find a mental stratagem to turn this fear into a feeling of pleasure. That is the best way to inspire you to do things, rather than forcing yourself. Examples: opt for an intense feeling of curiosity in other people; think about 'the game' and the challenges; or try to talk about topics which you hold dear.

• Distract your mind with something else:

Our brain cannot mull over a negative thought *("I'm worthless")* at the same time as another more stimulating thought *("Is my behaviour now innate or acquired?")*. It is either one or the other. Before you go out, occupy your thoughts by thinking about things which take your mind over – an existential question; your next meal; your favourite tune; a joke; 133 x 12 =? Etc.

• Think about other people before anything else:

This is the best way to proceed so that you do not remain focused on your unease. When meeting people, instead of seeing yourself as the centre of attention (an egocentric attitude), think about the other person's well-being first. Take a sincere interest in them and aim to please them (a thoughtful attitude). *"In my mind, HE/SHE must take priority over ME."*

INFO SHEET 20

HOW TO REACT TO MOCKERY

It might sometimes happen that you are mocked at work or school. You are different – you have particular physical characteristics or a disability, and occasionally your colleagues come out with hurtful or caustic comments about you.

This is a highly sensitive topic because these are exceedingly distressful situations over which you have no control and must endure through no fault of your own, without there being an ideal solution.

Inevitably, our morale is affected by others' gibes. Unfortunately, we shall never be able to eliminate that primary reflex which human beings have of mocking those who are different from themselves. It is a negative aspect of human nature – those who do not meet the group's norms are excluded.

Generally, the advice given is for one to learn to disregard mockery. This is because, if you respond, you tend to lend it weight; whereas people usually will get bored if they see no reaction from you to their cutting remarks.

However, indifference has its limits too. So, depending on the context, this is not the solution either!

Humour and educational methods remain the best weapons inasmuch as they allow you to save face and maintain ties with others.

A FEW TIPS
ON HOW TO DEAL WITH PEOPLE'S MOCKERY

● **Proudly accept that you are different:**
The first piece of advice is that you have to accept yourself as you are. This is because, if you feel uncomfortable with your individuality or if you have a permanent complex, then you will perceive every remark and passing reference made about you by your mates as an attack. However, they will not affect you if you are inwardly confident about your individuality – or at the very least... you do accept it!

Example of a reaction: *"Yes, I'm a rather introverted, quiet sort of a*

---

person. That's my personality and I've always been happy as I am. Why would you want me to change my nature?"

● **Use humour and self-deprecation:**

It goes without saying that this is not the easiest reaction to have when one is affected by other people's sarcasm! Nevertheless, we do not always have a choice and it is the only way to save face and downplay the situation. Show that you can laugh at your distinguishing features. Self-deprecation has a remarkable capacity to command respect from others and give them a better impression of you.

Here is an example given by an Internet user with a stammer: *"When people make fun of my stammer, I answer by saying, 'Ah, so, you, you you you you you no-no-no-noticed?' This makes people laugh and builds a rapport."*

● **Encourage people to put themselves in your position:**

People often stop their taunting when they finally understand the torment you endure. You can come back with hard-hitting retorts, such as the following:

▶ *"Just imagine that every time you came across someone, the only thing they could do is snigger and jeer at you. How would you react in my place?"*

▶ *"I do my best to fit in. If it were you who had these difficulties, how would you feel if I made fun of you? Would that encourage you to do your best?"*

▶ *"Yes, it's true I've got big ears. If it were your brother who had this problem, what would you feel deep down when you found out that everyone teased him?"*

▶ *"Remember that day when you yourself were being taunted and people were being nasty to you. How did you feel then?"*

● **Do a verbal presentation about your disability in front of the entire group:**

Ask your boss or schoolteacher to give you half an hour for you to do a verbal presentation about your 'difference' in front of your colleagues or school mates. The goal is for them have a better understanding of your disability. Relate your everyday life; explain your difficulties; help them to help you. It is a radical method but it can turn out to be effective because the whole group is attentive and can interact with you in order to find solutions together.

INFO SHEET 21

EXERCISES AND CHALLENGES TO REINVIGORATE YOUR SOCIAL RELATIONSHIPS

Here is a collection of potential solutions to encourage you to get closer to people or rebuild a genuine bond with your friends.

If, one day, you feel as though you are stagnating and need challenges in the form of little games to reinvigorate your relationships, feel free to reread this info sheet to dig out some ideas!

Jot down your challenge in a notebook or private diary and remember to set it in motion that very week at your next meetings. You might be in for some pleasant surprises in return, and people will certainly appreciate what you have done.

You can also do this in the form of games of drawing cards. Write down the challenges on cards or bits of paper; mix them up and draw a card which will be your challenge for the day...

Do, by all means, complete the list with your own ideas which align with your aspirations.

LIST OF EXAMPLES OF SOCIAL CHALLENGES:

- Contact a friend who you have not been in touch with for a year or so, to ask how they are.

- Deliver a six-minute monologue to a friend, talking about a favourite interest of yours or a project.

- Pay a sincere compliment to a work colleague or customer.

- Tell a friend or one of your nearest and dearest that you hold them in high esteem and that they matter to you.

- Suggest to an acquaintance who you would like to get to know better that you go out together.

- Tell a work colleague all about the most memorable journey you

---

have been on.

- Say thank you to someone to whom you feel you did not show sufficient gratitude in the past.

- Ask a friend what three things would please them.

- Be genuine. Open up to a friend about something which is worrying you at the moment.

- Express regret to a friend about things you would have liked to share with them more.

- Give one of your friends or relatives a chummy tap on the shoulder.

- Contact three or four friends and organise a group excursion which they might enjoy.

- Tell one of your friends an important secret about yourself.

- Suggest a project to a friend (a common goal, an association, a creative activity).

- Go to a new event and ask people what their dreams and interests are in life.

- Amongst your contacts, seek out a friend who is in need, and offer to do them a favour.

- Suggest playing this game of social challenges to someone it might benefit....

INFO SHEET 22

SETS OF QUESTIONS
TO PEP UP YOUR DISCUSSIONS

This last info sheet presents a set of ideas for questions to pep up your discussions and make them either more fun or more profound. The aim is to steer the conversation into areas which people do not necessarily expect, allowing you to connect with the other person.

Some people feel uncomfortable at the thought of using ready-made techniques and phrases but it is a pity to think in this way because the idea is only to draw inspiration from them! It is far better to have a few good ideas in your mind and try them out to see what happens, rather than remaining passive and reproducing the same unproductive conversations.

We underestimate the power of questions and their positive impact. A single sentence is sometimes enough to make a conversation more lively, allowing it to reach beyond the scope of a pre-agreed or formal discussion. That is the whole purpose of this info sheet.

We can turn this into a set of questions. To paraphrase the Reverend Doctor Richard Lingard, *"You can discover more about a person in an hour of play than in a year of conversation."*

HERE IS A LIST OF INSPIRATIONAL QUESTIONS:

- Who is your favourite superhero and why?
- Tell me all about the dream place where you'd like to live.
- How would your best friend describe you?
- For which noble cause in this world would you be prepared to fight?
- What question have you been asking yourself most recently?
- What is the strangest thing you've ever experienced?
- If you could have three wishes fulfilled, what would they be?
- What in your opinion makes you so different?
- What would you do if you had the power to be invisible whenever you want?
- What kind of friends would you like to have?
- Tell me about your three favourite books or films.

- If your life were to end at midnight what would your greatest regret be?
- Which celebrity do you admire the most?
- Tell me a little secret!
- What qualities do your friends have in common?
- What three moments in your life have the most importance?
- What do you think about spirituality? Do you believe in the paranormal?
- If you won the lottery, what would you do with the money?
- Tell me three things you could teach me.
- What compliments have you received of which you were most proud?
- What music best suits your personality?
- If you could relive a time in your life, what would it be?
- Name three accomplishments in your life of which you are proud.
- What things in life readily bring a smile to your face?
- Have you ever dreamt of being famous? If so, in what field?
- When you think of your future, what pleasant images come to mind?
- If you had to write a book about your life, which chapters would stand out?

SUMMARY

REVIEW YOUR SOCIAL COMMUNICATION

SITUATIONS	STAGES	TICK BOXES
AT AN EVENT (MEETING, PARTY, ETC.)	**SHOWING PEOPLE MY SIGNS OF AVAILABILITY:**	**I know how to do this**
	Physically approaching the person	
	Looking people in the eye	
	Speaking in a clear voice	
	Smiling	
	Having an open body posture	
	Having a welcoming demeanour	

Things to remember: Do not worry if you feel stressed or awkward. The main thing is that you have shown the other person you are approachable.

AT AN INTERACTION OR MEETING	**SHOWING THE OTHER PERSON MY SIGNS OF SOCIABILITY:**	**I know how to do this**
	Having an open, friendly look	
	Having a winning smile	
	Keeping a conversation going	
	Having friendly physical contact	
	Taking a sincere interest in others	
	Having a positive mood and a sense of humour	
	Paying a sincere compliment	
	Knowing how to be conciliatory with others	
	Expressing one's gratitude to others	
	Taking initiatives; inviting people	

Things to remember: You need not master every sign of sociability all at once, only those which are in line with your personality.

IN A GROUP SITUATION	USING AVAILABLE SOCIAL COMMUNICATION	I know how to do this
	Smiling	
	Showing signs of approval	
	Asking questions	
	Rephrasing what the other person has said	
	Being attentive	
	Showing yourself to be receptive to friendly advances	

Things to remember: We do forgive those extremely introverted people who know how to appear accessible – but not those who deliberately shut off their social communication.

CLOSING WORDS:
THINGS TO CONTEMPLATE...

A FEW SECONDS TO SHOW OUR BENEVOLENCE

"We spend hours and expend our energy working, doing household chores, surfing the Internet, dwelling on the days passing by, and so on."

"Why could we not just take one minute to display our signs of sociability to other people in the most positive way?"

"A genuine smile, a warm embrace, a sincere compliment, expression of one's gratitude to another, offering one's help, etc."

"Few of us truly do this with our friends and loved ones. We only think of talking, of keeping the conversation going, whilst periods of silence leave room for a 'magic phrase' which can lead a human interaction in quite a different direction."

"The truth is that these little routines often take only a few seconds. They can shake up our interactions from the bourgeoning of a friendship or the reinvigoration of a relationship, right through to helping there to be more social harmony in society."

Sylvain Zelliot

ABOUT THE AUTHOR

Sylvain Zelliot is a writer, blogger and coach for atypical people.

It has always been his aspiration to create a bible of social relations so that people can be calmer and happier when interacting with others.

On his blog, Striving for Social Harmony, visited by more than ten thousand Internet users every month, he provides his expertise on the subjects of shyness and introversion through hundreds of articles and helpful tools.

Feel free to contact me by email: sylvain.zelliot@gmail.com

HOW TO THANK ME
AND GIVE ME SOLID SUPPORT

If you have enjoyed my guide, remember to support me by giving me publicity on your social networks and/or by writing a positive comment on the book's Amazon page. This will only take you a minute and will help me a great deal in making my book better known.

It has taken me almost three years of hard work to write the book, do all the diagrams and compile hundreds of practical examples for the info sheets. Often, people do not think of leaving a comment to support a book they have enjoyed and yet, this can really help an author. Be assured that I would be delighted and touched to receive your support!

Should you have any critical comments, please send them to me directly rather than publishing them on the Amazon page because this could adversely affect my guide and discourage potential readers. I will consider any constructive criticism as a means to self-improvement and shall look into every idea put forward. ☺

BIBLIOGRAPHY AND REFERENCES

ANDRE, Christophe & LEGERON, Patrick - *Fear of Others*, Editions Odile Jacob, 1998.

ANDRE, Christophe - *Psychology of Fear*, Editions Odile Jacob, 2004.

ATTWOOD, Tony - *Asperger's Syndrome, The Complete Guide* – Editions De Boeck, 2010.

BENGLIA, Jean-Paul - *The Love Encounter within Everyone's Reach*, Editions Tatamis, 2011.

BOST, Cecile - *Difference and Suffering of the Gifted Adult,* Editions Vuibert, 2011.

CAIN, Susan – *Quiet: The Power of Introverts*, Editions JC Lattès, 2013.

CHAPMAN, Gary – *The Five Love Languages*, Editions Farel, 1997.

CUNGI, Charly - *Overcoming Shyness*, Guide (Broché), Editions Retz, 2010.

CYRULNIK, Boris - *Resilience*, Editions Fabert, Collection Penser le monde de l'enfant, 2009.

DAN, Yu - *Happiness according to Confucius*, Editions Belfond, 2009.

FILLIOZAT, Isabelle – *The Intelligence of the Heart*, Marabout, 2013.

GOFFMAN, Erving - *Interaction Ritual*, Editions de Minuit, Le sens commun, 1974.

GOFFMAN, Erving - *Stigma*, Editions de Minuit, Le sens commun, 1975.

GORDON, Thomas - *The Gordon Method*, (P.E.T. in Action), 1976.

GRANOVETTER, Mark - *The Strength of Weak Ties*, Sociological Theory Vol. 1, 1983.

MARTIN, Jean-Claude – *The Communication Guide*, Editions Marabout, 1999.

N. ARON, Elaine - *The Highly Sensitive Person*, Editions de l'Homme, 2013.

TEYSSEDRE, Anne - *The Keys to Animal Communication*, Editions Delachaux et Niestle, 2006.

[1] Egocentric speech is the child's first language, involving the child talking to him or herself. The psychologist Lev Vygotsky considered egocentric speech to be initially social, subsequently becoming a tool for building thought.

[2] In his book, *Psychologie de la Peur* (The Psychology of Fear), Dr. Christophe André suggests a number of avenues for reflection inspired by the research of evolutionist psychology into the origin of phobias, shyness and anxiety attacks.

[3] How to Win Friends and Influence People is a book by the writer Dale Carnegie which was published in 1936. He was born in 1888 and died in 1955.

[4] The need for social belonging according to Maslow (1970) is part of the five groups of fundamental human needs: physiological needs, safety needs, love and belonging needs, esteem needs, and self-actualisation needs.

[5] Scientific studies into solitude: many studies highlighting an obvious connection between isolation and mental health are referenced here: https://en.wikipedia.org/wiki/Solitude

[6] Harvard study into happiness and social ties. Robert Waldinger's report. Source: https://news.harvard.edu/gazette/story/2017/04/over-nearly-80-years-harvard-study-has-been-showing-how-to-live-a-healthy-and-happy-life/

[7] Carl Jung was the first to give a definition of the word *introvert* in his book "Psychological Types" in 1913. According to him, the introverted type is defined by energy orientated towards a person's inner world.

[8] This is an estimation of the population of introverts, formulated by Susan Cain in her book, *Quiet: The Power of Introverts*, and based on MBTI (Myers Briggs Type Indicator) research.

[9] Dr. Christophe André uses the expression, 'a biologically upset Internal Alarm System' in his book *Psychologie de la Peur* (The Psychology of Fear) to explain the root cause of the distress felt by a person suffering from social phobia. He likens it to an allergic reaction with its attendant immune hyperactivity.

[10] Psychologist Jerome Kagan (The Nature of the Child, 1984) has carried out longitudinal research on children aged 4 months, 2, 4, 7 and 11 years old. He has concluded that predispositions to temperament, inhibited or otherwise, exist in children from birth.

[11] Williams or Williams-Beuren Syndrome (WS), discovered in 1961 by New Zealand cardiologist J.C.P. Williams, and described in 1962 by German paediatrician A.J. Beuren. The disorder is due to a deletion of a number of genes.

[12] Psychodiversity: Dr. André uses this term in *Comment Gérer les Personnalités Difficiles* (2000) and lists a collection of personality types who have a different psychological profile. He attempts to explain their origin with inspiration drawn from evolutionist psychology.

[13] Psychologist Elaine Aron provides an overview of the main characteristics of the hypersensitive person in, The Highly Sensitive Person: How to Thrive When the World Overwhelms You, New York, Birch Lane Press, 1997.

[14] An individual is said to be intellectually gifted when their IQ exceeds 130, as measured by the WISC or WAIS. The threshold of 130 corresponds to two standard deviations above average, by symmetry with the definition of mental retardation (IQ under 70, being two standard deviations under average). This represents 2.2% of the population on which the test has been calibrated.

[15] Asperger's Syndrome is a form of autism which was defined clinically by Lorna Wing in 1981, on the basis of autistic psychopathy described by Dr. Hans Asperger in 1944. It was subsequently included in official ICD-10 and DSM nosographic classifications in the 1990s.

[16] *The Top Five Regrets of the Dying* is a book written by Bronnie Ware, an Australian nurse, published in 2011. She cared for sick people at the end of their lives and wrote down their last words.

[17] Boris Cyrulnik popularised the concept of resilience (1990) following John Bowlby's research into attachment theory and observation of concentration camp survivors.

[18] Study by Jean-Claude Martin, *Le Guide de la Communication* (1999), chap. II, Le Regard.

[19] Ron Gutman presents the findings of his studies into the positive, contagious power of smiling in the article, *The Untapped Power of Smiling* (2011) in Forbes magazine.

[20] Source: the magazine, *"Pour la Science"*: https://www.pourlascience.fr/theme/pouvoir-du-toucher/le-toucher-un-facteur-cle-dans-les-interactions-sociales-8872.php

[21] The Kleinke Experiment (1977), published in the Journal of Experimental Social Psychology.

[22] Source: Introduction to Psychology, Rod Plotnik, Universal Facial Expressions, p. 364, Motivation & Emotion.

[23] Studies by Dr. Emmons & Dr. McCullough (2003), Evidence of the benefits of gratitude. Source : https://www.passeportsante.net/fr/psychologie/Fiche.aspx?doc=gratitude

[24] Altruism activates the areas of the brain associated with a feeling of happiness: https://www.sciencesetavenir.fr/sante/cerveau-et-psy/la-generosite-rend-votre-cerveau-heureux_114722

[25] Cerebral plasticity is one of the recent discoveries in neuroscience: "Le cerveau, comment il se réorganise sans cesse" (How the brain constantly reorganises itself). Les Dossiers de la Recherche, No. 40, August, 2010.

Manufactured by Amazon.ca
Bolton, ON

37114411R00122